"Oppression reproduces itself anew each day, requiring us to continually adapt our tools of resistance. *Beautiful Rising* offers insights and lessons for creative resistance from across the Global South, making it a crucial resource for changemakers."

—Archbishop Desmond Tutu, educator and civil rights activist

"Tom Hayden once said that change is slow except when it's fast. We're in a fast mo right now when the creative storytelling, strategizing, and organizing we do really m *Beautiful Rising* inspires and teaches by offering access to some of the most tactica imaginative ways people can turn the resources they have into the power they neec achieve the change they want — around the world."

—Marshall Ganz, author of *Why David Sometimes Wins: Leadership, Organization, and Strategy in the California Farm Worker Movement*

"Syrian activists evaded the soldier and censor by releasing hundreds of ping pong covered in liberatory messages to bounce through the streets of Damascus . . . In the same spirit, *Beautiful Rising* bounces dozens of these and other stories, tactics, strategies, theories, and inspiration from social movements across the Global South into the public square of ideas. May they roll everywhere and be picked up by curious hands to play with."

—Katherine Ainger, co-editor of *We Are Everywhere: The Irresistible Rise of Global Anti-Capitalism*

"*Beautiful Rising* is an extraordinary treasury of insights and lessons from some of the world's savviest grassroots movements. Prepare to be inspired by the creativity and resilience showcased in this smart, exuberant volume, created through a remarkable collaboration among organizers from around the globe."

—L.A. Kauffman, author of *Direct Action: Protest and the Reinvention of American Radicalism*

"Time and time over we are seeing our local struggles uniting globally. From Palestine to Mexico, *Beautiful Rising* is making this connection more explicit and urgent."

—Rafeef Ziadah, poet and human rights activist

"Beyond a brilliantly innovative toolkit for making social change, you will find here a 'deep structure' of activist patterns and principles that can unite millions in creating a new world beyond capitalist sociopathy and strong man despotism. Read this optimistic book for hope in grim times."

—Charles Derber, author of *Welcome to the Revolution: Universalizing Resistance for Social Justice* and *Democracy in Perilous Times*

BEAUTIFUL RISING

CREATIVE RESISTANCE FROM THE GLOBAL SOUTH

BEAUTIFUL RISING

CREATIVE RESISTANCE FROM THE GLOBAL SOUTH

edited by

JUMAN ABUJBARA

ANDREW BOYD

DAVE MITCHELL

MARCEL TAMINATO

O/R

OR Books

New York • London

beautifulrising.org

Any and all author proceeds from the sale of this book will go towards fulfilling the mission of the Beautiful Rising project as a whole, including, but not limited to, supporting and facilitating the work of grassroots movements worldwide.

Published by OR Books, New York and London
Visit our website at *orbooks.com*

Library of Congress Cataloging-in-Publication Data: A catalog record for this book is available from the Library of Congress. British Library Cataloguing-in-Publication Data: A catalog record for this book is available from the British Library.

Book design by The Public Society
thepublicsociety.com

ISBN 978-1-94486-981-6 paperback
ISBN 978-1-68219-113-2 ebook

II

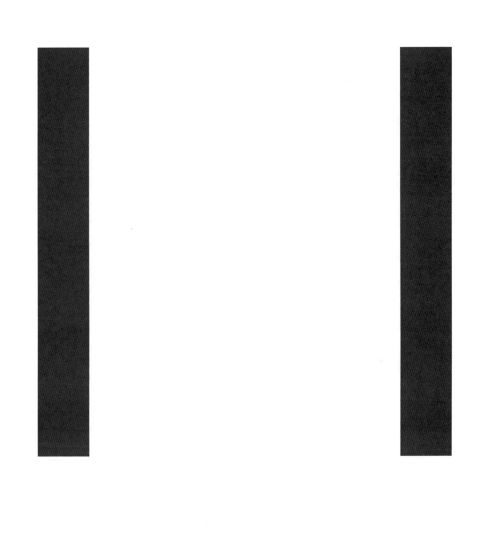

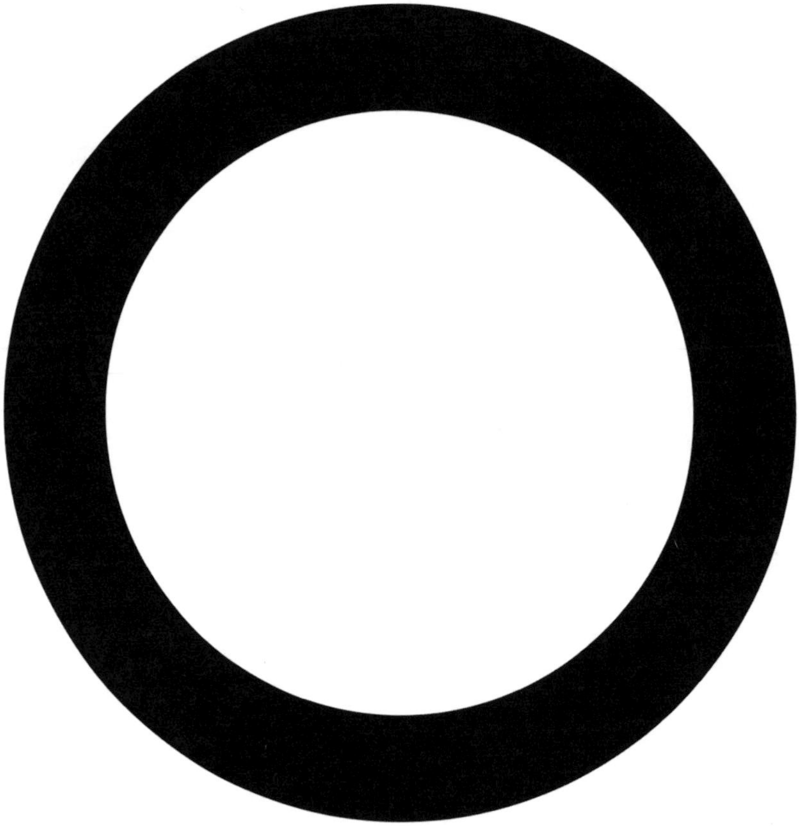

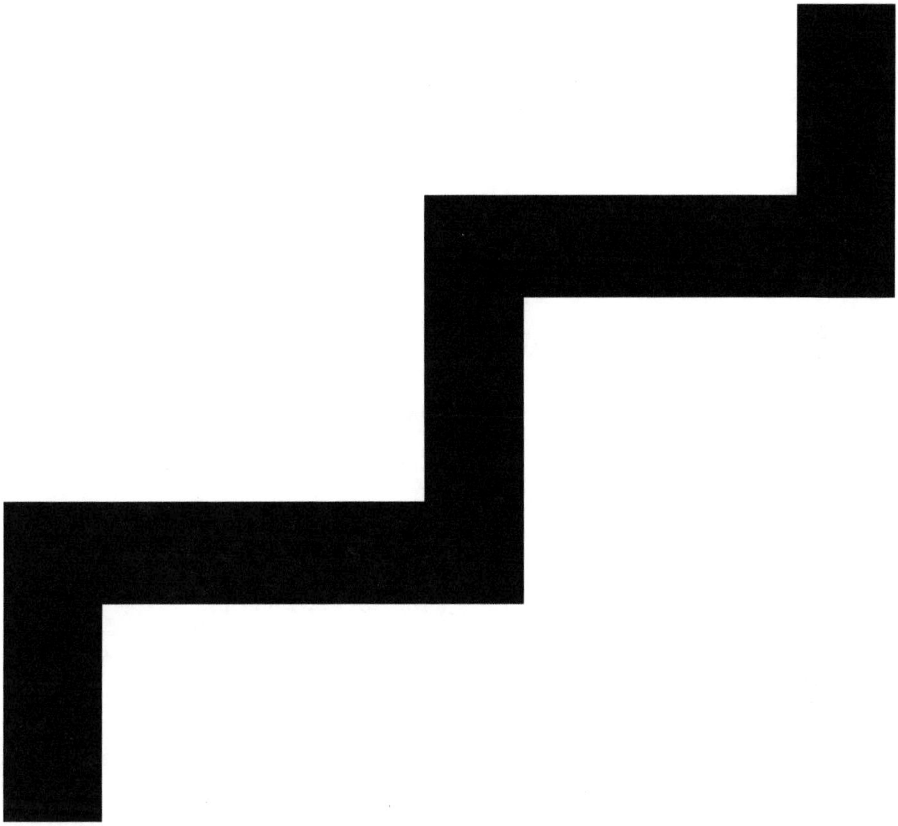

FOREWORD

THE PLANETARY SATYAGRAHA

Vandana Shiva

Humanity stands at an evolutionary crossroads. We can consciously choose the path of oneness — one planet, one humanity, celebrating our many diversities and our interconnectedness — or we can cling to illusions of security and stability while our real ecological security is undermined and our real social security is broken through the politics of division, hate, and fear.

The planet and humanity face the same enemy: the 1%, which is destroying the genius of nature and humanity, enclosing the commons, and spawning poverty and dispossession. We can defeat the 1%'s mechanical mind by becoming aware of our relationships with the Earth and with each other. This awareness enlarges our being, our potential, and our power, thereby rendering the emergence of a radical shift possible.

As we tend to these relationships, we become aware that rejuvenating the planet and reclaiming our humanity are not two different ends, reached through different paths, because the Earth and society are interwoven in one indivisible, vibrant, colorful fabric of life in autopoetic freedom. We will either make peace with the Earth by realizing that we are part of her, and not her masters, owners, or conquerors, or the Earth will make our continued existence increasingly difficult.

Beautiful Rising is grounded in this premise of interconnectedness. By compiling a common platform to document the most effective approaches and latest innovations in creative activism from the Global South, *Beautiful Rising* responds to the needs of diverse movements in a spirit of horizontal, open, and participatory collaboration. These teachings invite us to open new, democratic spaces at a time when those available to us are shrinking; to cultivate compassion and solidarity in times of greed, fear, and hate; and to reclaim our collective strength.

Over the past four and a half decades of my service to the Earth, I have always turned to Gandhi's teachings for inspiration. His struggle for freedom from the British Empire teaches us that true freedom and wealth creation call for the practice of *satyagraha, swaraj,* and *swadeshi.*

Satyagraha — the force of truth — is the moral duty to not cooperate with exploitative and undemocratic processes that destroy the Earth and rob us of our humanity and our freedoms. Non-cooperation is the first step in breaking free from the enslaving shackles of colonialism.

Swaraj — self-organization, self-rule, self-governance — is the basis of real freedom in nature and society, beginning at the smallest level, then emerging at higher levels. Resistance by itself does not create freedom from oppression. Resistance without constructive action will not create another world. Only by sowing the seeds of freedom do we become one with the Earth and one with our own nature.

Swadeshi is self-support. It involves local production of our basic needs based on local resources, indigenous knowledge, and community. It makes possible the expression of our fullest creativity as Earth citizens. In swadeshi, we are co-creative with nature's intelligence and regenerative potential. It is not extractive, polluting, or degrading to the planet or to human communities. It is the foundation of sustainability, the core of economic democracy, and the source of well-being and happiness for all.

The freedoms we enjoy today are the fruits of the struggles of our ancestors and forebearers, who refused to co-operate with unjust laws that denied us our full humanity — whether it was slavery in the United States, racial segregation in South Africa, or the colonization of India. Higher moral laws compel citizens to disobey laws that institutionalize injustice and violence. Our freedoms are gifts of civil disobedience and satyagraha.

In 1848, Henry David Thoreau coined the term *civil disobedience* in his essay on why his commitment to the abolition of slavery led to his refusal to pay the poll tax. Satyagraha was, and has always been, about awakening our conscience, our inner power to resist external, brute power. Satyagraha, the force of truth, is more important than ever in our "post-truth" age. It is an autopoetic response to the cruel and unjust global system imposed upon us. As Gandhi said, satyagraha is a *no* said from our deepest conscience.

Breaking free of the 1% is the satyagraha of our times. Today's non-cooperation movement begins with not subscribing to the fictions and falsehoods through which we are colonized, and not cooperating with the regimes of violence and domination that enforce systematic extraction and exploitation. It is the contours of this emerging planetary satyagraha that *Beautiful Rising* is painting through its documentation of concrete and creative struggles and its celebration of the perennial urge for freedom and life.

INTRODUCTION

Juman Abujbara, Andrew Boyd, Dave Mitchell, and Marcel Taminato

The defining challenges of our era — deepening inequality, erosion of civil rights, and compounding disasters linked to climate change and war — cannot be adequately addressed by business-as-usual politics. The neoliberal consensus has nothing to offer the vast majority of the world's people; only sustained, people-powered social movements can lead us through this catastrophe. Grassroots movements the world over are responding with astounding courage and creativity, even in the face of unspeakable violence. But to actually win, these social movements need ways to share, analyze, and learn from one another. That is precisely what the Beautiful Rising project seeks to offer.[1]

1 A partnership between ActionAid, a Global South-based NGO, and Beautiful Trouble (beautifultrouble.org), an international activist training and publishing collective, the Beautiful Rising project includes a multilingual toolbox of creative organizing principles and practices. This book is a selection of pieces from the full toolbox available at beautifulrising.org, which you can also access through our chatbot and strategy game at beautifulrising.org/platforms.

Towards a "pattern language" of social change

Beautiful Rising is a modular and interlinking toolkit for social change, rooted in the concept of a *pattern language*. As the originator of the pattern language concept, Christopher Alexander, explains: "A pattern describes a problem which occurs over and over again in our environment, and then describes the core of the solution to that problem, in such a way that you can use this solution a million times over, without ever doing it the same way twice." Pattern languages offer flexible, democratic, and endlessly adaptable solutions to common challenges, and have been developed for fields as varied as computer science, media studies, and group decision-making. Here, we have adapted the model to the field of social change. We've identified five types of social change tools that, together, offer organizers a strategic framework to adapt to their own unique circumstances:

Stories:
Accounts of memorable actions and campaigns, analyzing what worked (or didn't) and why.

Tactics:
Specific forms of creative action, such as a flash mob or blockade.

Principles:
Time-tested guidelines for how to design successful actions and campaigns.

Theories:
Big-picture ideas that help us understand how the world works and how we might change it.

Methodologies:
Strategic frameworks and hands-on exercises to help assess our situation and plan a campaign.

This is an open-ended undertaking. As new movements arise, new stories must be told, new insights gleaned, new tactics, principles, theories, and methodologies developed. The toolkit evolves alongside the movements that use it on the ground, providing organizers with a responsive framework for thinking about their own efforts alongside others' stories of success or failure. Because this book represents just a subset of the evolving collection of tools, in the following pages we will sometimes reference tools that are not published here but can be found in the online toolkit at beautifulrising.org.

Lessons and insights

Over a hundred organizers from five continents have contributed to the platform, many of them through face-to-face jam sessions we held in Yangon, Amman, Harare, Dhaka, Kampala, and Oaxaca in 2015 and 2016. The stories they shared include the Ugandan organizers who protested corruption with *Yellow Pigs in Parliament* (p. 96), the *Burmese Students' Long March* against undemocratic and overly centralized education reforms in 2015 (p. 26), the Lebanese *Honk at Parliament* campaign against politicians who had clung to power long after their term had expired (p. 44), and many others.

What emerged from this process was a global network of frontline organizers, theorists, and strategists documenting innovations and analyzing common challenges. Among these challenges, the issue of the *NGO-ization of resistance* (p. 200) — the ways in which the rapid proliferation of non-governmental organizations under neoliberalism has inhibited popular and democratic struggles — quickly revealed itself as a problem faced by activists working in vastly different contexts across Asia, Africa, and Latin America. By naming it, changemakers were able to identify a key pattern across their various struggles and thus better target neoliberalism as a global repressive ideology. To counter this destructive force, activists identified a need for *solidarity not aid* — both south-south solidarity, and a rebalancing of the power dynamics of north-south solidarity *(see PRINCIPLE: Solidarity not aid).*

The growing ferocity of state violence is another challenge faced by activists across the Global South. In response, activists shared several principles that guide their work and help to ensure their safety, such as *seeking safety in support networks* (p. 150) in order to deter state and paramilitary violence, and *jail solidarity* (p. 118) to deter abuse and shorten the detention of imprisoned activists.

While many common global challenges were revealed, other challenges seemed particular to a country or region — for example, the use of *baltajiah* (thugs) (p. 176) by authoritarian regimes in the Middle East to repress rising movements. Though it's called different names in different countries (in Jordan and Palestine, *sahijeh* or "clappers"; in Egypt, *baltajiah* or "axes"; in Syria, *shabiha* or "ghosts"), a common political formation was identified by activists across the region: a marginalized group that are paid to support the state apparatus in key moments by violently disrupting movements seeking change. One of the most famous manifestations of this phenomenon is the *Battle of the Camel* (p. 14), in which camel riders attacked and killed protesters in Egypt's Tahrir Square in 2011.

In the process of documenting the creative methods used by movements operating in politically repressive environments, we often uncovered similar patterns of creative response that had very different expressions from country to country. Take, for example, *clandestine leafleting*, a way to share information with the public when it's too dangerous to do so openly *(see TACTIC: Clandestine leafleting at beautifulrising.org)*. In Syria, activists sent a cascade of slogan-marked ping-pong balls bouncing through the streets, and in Myanmar (Burma) they wafted a fleet of leaflet-laden hot-air lanterns across the city.

Throughout our workshops, campaigners repeatedly called for better tools to facilitate strategic thinking. To address this need, contributors documented the strategic frameworks and hands-on exercises their organizations use to assess their situation and plan their campaigns. The best of these are collected in the *methodologies* section.

We hope this book, and the larger project of which it is a part, will serve as an evolving body of knowledge for veteran social change practitioners, as well as an effective entry point for newcomers into the incredible creativity with which social movements are building resistance across the Global South. Since the platform launched online, more and more people have been getting in touch to contribute ideas, share lessons, request trainings, strategize local campaigns, and build a stronger global network of solidarity among changemakers. We hope this will only continue in the years ahead.

Finally, we'll leave you with choice words from novelist and activist Arundhati Roy, from which this work draws much inspiration:

"Our strategy should be not only to confront Empire but to lay siege to it. To deprive it of oxygen. To shame it. To mock it. With our art, our music, our literature, our stubbornness, our joy, our brilliance, our sheer relentlessness — and our ability to tell our own stories. Stories that are different from the ones we're being brainwashed to believe.

The corporate revolution will collapse if we refuse to buy what they are selling — their ideas, their version of history, their wars, their weapons, their notion of inevitability.

Remember this: We be many and they be few. They need us more than we need them.[2] "

2 Arundhati Roy, *The End of Imagination* (Chicago: Haymarket Books, 2016).

HOW TO READ THIS BOOK

Beautiful Rising is not a traditional book. It's a network of interrelated concepts or *tools* that you can read in any order.

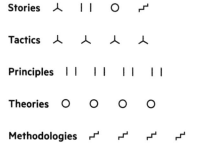

There are five types of tools in the *Beautiful Rising* toolbox: *stories, tactics, principles, theories,* and *methodologies.*

Each type of tool has a designated symbol:

Stories ⅄ | | O ⌐

Tactics ⅄ ⅄ ⅄ ⅄

Principles | | | | | | | |

Theories O O O O

Methodologies ⌐ ⌐ ⌐ ⌐

Each tool begins with a snapshot summary. Each tool ends by listing one or more *key* and *related* tools. You can think of a *key* tool as helping to explain the current tool through the eyes of other tools from the toolbox. For example, let's say you are reading the tactic *civil disobedience* (p. 108). In the write-up, you will find the key principle *maintain nonviolent discipline* and a paragraph explaining how nonviolent discipline informs a successful civil disobedience effort. You will also find a list of related tools that you can refer to if you want to gain a broader understanding on the uses of civil disobedience.

⚠ **Potential risks**
If you see this sign, know that there are some risks or potential pitfalls involved that you need to be aware of.

Online toolbox
Because this book represents just a subset of a much larger and still expanding set of tools in the online toolbox, you will sometimes see a reference to a tool that is not published in the book, but can be found online at beautifulrising.org.

(see: NAME OF TOOL)
You may see (*see: NAME OF TOOL*) in the text you are reading. It will either be followed by a page number or it won't. If it does include a page number, you can simply turn to that page. If it does not, you can find the tool in the online toolbox.

Learn more
Each tool also lists a few resources under the heading "Learn More." Rather than providing a long URL for readers to type into their browser to find the resource, we have opted to provide just enough information to allow you to find the resource using an online search. (Alternatively, you can go to our online toolbox and simply click the hotlinked resource you're looking for.)

Contribute
Finally, if you have an idea for a tool that you would like to see included in the toolbox, we'd love to hear from you. Please submit your story, tactic, principle, theory, or methodology at beautifulrising.org/contribute.

STORIES

Accounts of memorable actions and campaigns, analyzing what worked (or didn't) and why.

"Sometimes you win, sometimes you learn."
—Anonymous

Revolutionaries practice without safety nets. Our laboratory is the world around us – the streets, the Internet, the airwaves, our own hearts. We experiment, we fail, we readjust, we try again, maybe this time a little less disastrously, a little more beautifully – until eventually, we win. Always we learn. In these stories we share what we've learned.

BATTLE OF THE CAMEL

Tahrir Square, Cairo, Egypt | *2-3 February, 2011*

A violent attack on protesters in Tahrir Square by pro-regime, camel-riding thugs was a turning point in the Egyptian revolution, generating popular support for the protesters and leading to the fall of Mubarak.

Loay Bakr

On February 2, 2011, in a desperate attempt to disrupt the masses of protesters who were occupying Cairo's central Tahrir Square, thousands of *baltajiah* (thugs) attacked protesters using stones, knives, and Molotov cocktails. Many rode camels, mules, and horses and used swords, sticks, and whips to attack the demonstrators. New fighting erupted again the next day involving live ammunition and rubber bullets.

Preliminary reports of a post-revolutionary fact-finding committee found that key members of the regime were behind the baltajiah who led this battle, demonstrating once again how convenient it is for those in power to get civilian thugs to do their dirty work for them.

Though the aim of the attack was to abort the revolution, quite the opposite happened. The attack instead provoked a massive wave of sympathy and support. The murder of nearly a dozen protesters and the wounding of 2,000 others created a public outcry, which led millions of people to take to the streets and join the Tahrir Square sit-in, forcing decades-long dictator Hosni Mubarak to step down nine days later.

The Battle of the Camel was a turning point in the Egyptian revolution. But it could have gone either way. What factors caused it to be a victory for the people? One was the resilience and bravery of the protesters. The thugs were each paid 200 Egyptian pounds to carry out the attacks, but the protesters' strong belief in their right to "bread, freedom, and social justice" was much sturdier than any monetary incentive. They not only held their ground, but also capitalized on the attack to expand and escalate the revolution.

For the first seven days of the occupation of the square there was no indication that the regime was willing to compromise. People were beginning to feel that their efforts were not bearing any fruit. But the attack showed that the regime was hysterical and had run out of options *(see: PRINCIPLE: The real action is your target's reaction)*. Despite the blood in the streets, it gave protesters a huge morale boost.

The protesters began calling upon their friends and relatives, marching through the alleyways, pleading with their Egyptian brothers and sisters to come to their

"The people had answered the plight of the people."

This Chris Hondros/Getty image effectively dramatized the clash between protestors and baltajiah, helping to galvanize popular opposition to the Mubarak regime in a crucial phase of the uprising.

rescue. And they did. The brutality of the regime provoked hundreds of thousands who were sitting on the fence and watching the revolution from afar to take to the streets and join the sit-in in Tahrir Square *(see: PRINCIPLE: Anger works best when you have the moral high ground).*

At dawn of February 2, there were 30,000 thugs and 25,000 protesters. By the afternoon, the number of protesters reached 300,000, and by nightfall there were a million protesters in the streets of Egypt. The people had answered the plight of the people in a surge of solidarity *(see: THEORY: Al faza'a [a surge of solidarity] p. 172).*

WHY IT WORKED

Protesters turned a threat into an opportunity. They rightly saw the attack as a way to discredit the regime, generate sympathy for the protesters, and massively escalate the revolution. They used many different creative means to call upon the people to rise up: social media to share images of the attack and expose the brutality of the regime, and songs, poetry, and music — both online and off — to inspire people to take action. International media broadcast live from Tahrir Square, and protesters issued status updates every 30 minutes. People were already following the developments in real time and felt part of what was happening when they were asked to switch from observer to participant.

WHY IT FAILED

The reasons Egyptians took to the streets are many. But, the single most compelling reason was that people wanted to live in dignity. They wanted an end to corruption, totalitarianism, and decades-long dictatorship. They also wanted social justice and honorable standards of living. The main slogan of the revolution was "bread, freedom, and social justice." The viciousness of the regime during the Battle of the Camel channelled people's anger into a single, much-narrower demand: Mubarak, step down! When he did, we thought we had won, and it distracted us from our deeper demands and aspirations. Today, Mubarak is gone, but people are still hungry and the new regime is more corrupt and brutal than ever.

continued on next page ›

KEY TACTIC

OCCUPATION

Occupying Tahrir Square was a geographically and politically strategic move. The square is located in the geographical center of Cairo and is a focal entry and exit point. It disrupted business-as-usual not only for local shops and vendors, but also tourism, one of Egypt's main sources of income. Politically, having millions of people united under one demand was unprecedented for Egypt, and having them all gathered in the square showcased their numerical strength. Thus, the occupation of the square exceeded the threshold of acceptable risk for the regime. For 18 days, Tahrir Square became home to many protesters. Tents were erected, controlled points of entry were created, and revolutionary music concerts were held. What helped make this tactic sustainable was the generosity of the people living around the square, who opened their houses for protesters to wash, eat, and rest.

KEY PRINCIPLE

THE REAL ACTION IS YOUR TARGET'S REACTION

During the first week of the revolution, there was no indication that the regime was willing to heed the demands of the people. Many of us felt that the sleepless nights we were spending in Tahrir Square were a waste of time and should come to an end. But the Battle of the Camel changed our mood, as well as the mood of the entire country. The Egyptian people's response to the battle took the regime by surprise; it was clear they were reacting to the situation rather than containing it. The only interpretation was that the regime had run out of options and was effectively in a fight-or-flight mode. Now we knew: The harder we fought, the closer Mubarak was to fleeing.

RELATED

Al faza'a (a surge of solidarity) » *p. 172*
Baltajiah (thugs) » *p. 176*
Postcolonialism » *p. 196*

Pillars of power » *p. 210*
Spectrum of allies » *p. 232*

KEY THEORY

BALTAJIAH

The Battle of the Camel is one of the most infamous examples of baltajiah in action. A marginalized group was paid an insignificant amount of money to attack the protestors. The regime tried to distance itself from the thugs by claiming that they were loyalists who were supporting Mubarak's rule. When it became evident that the regime's hands were soaked in blood, people were provoked. There was no room left for justification. Furthermore, the thugs could not sustain their attack when they themselves had to pay the price.

Also, it became too expensive for the regime and some of its supporters from the velvet class to fund 25,000 thugs. And so, they vanished.

KEY METHODOLOGY

SPECTRUM OF ALLIES

The Battle of the Camel truly shifted the spectrum of allies and moved many of those who were on the fence (both inactive supporters and neutral people) to actually join the revolution. And this made all the difference. For the first week, tens of thousands of Egyptians were merely observers of the revolution. They preferred going about their daily lives without disruptions or were too comfortable behind the screen watching history. However, when protesters capitalized on the incident of the Battle of the Camel, and spoke to people's hearts and minds by exposing and highlighting the brutality of the regime, the people who had previously been inactive and neutral suddenly felt they had something bigger to lose. Quickly, people of different classes, ideologies, and backgrounds took to the streets and joined the revolution.

LEARN MORE

Egypt Revolution Turns Ugly as Mubarak Fights Back | The Guardian, 2011

Egypt Speaker "Plotted Battle of the Camel" | Al Jazeera, 2011

The Battle of the Camel: The Final Straw to Mubarak's Regime | Daily News Egypt, 2013

BOXING GENDER OPPRESSION

Nairobi, Kenya | *2008-present*

After Kenya's post-election violence in 2008, when many young women were sexually abused and traumatized, Boxgirls Kenya used boxing to fight the shaming, stigma, and fear they experienced.

"We are as small as the hummingbird, but we are focused, effective, and unstoppable risk takers."
—Boxgirls

Hope Chigudu

After Kenya's post-election violence in 2008, when many young women were sexually abused and traumatized, an organization called Boxgirls Kenya began using boxing as a strategic entry point for providing young women with a powerful antidote to the shaming, stigma, and fear generated by the oppression that they experience.

Most of the young women living in the slums of Nairobi, Kenya, are children of rural migrants. Their parents are often away most of the day for work, leaving young girls to care for themselves and their siblings; the schools are poorly equipped; there are no facilities or activities for young people. All this leads to a situation where young women are vulnerable to sexual abuse.

In response, many have found in boxing a safe space to learn self-defense and an entry point for addressing issues related to sex and sexuality, leadership skills, money management, health, and well-being. Boxing has proven to be a powerful tool for equipping girls and young women to protect themselves and ensure their security while boosting self-esteem and building confidence. The initiative has even trained the first female Olympic boxer in Kenyan history, Elizabeth Andiego.

This work has been led by a community-based organization called Boxgirls Kenya, which aims to empower young women to understand the insecurities they

"We use boxing to free girls and young women from fear."

From "Fragile Strength," a portrait series by Patricia Esteve.

are exposed to and to discuss strategies for dealing with them, so they can grow up free to love themselves. Boxgirls speaks movingly of the role boxing plays in the bout for a better world:

> *"Boxing is a strategy, power, and knowledge framework that creates an alternative world in which girls and young women's bodies are protected and their security assured. We use it to free girls and young women from fear."*

Participants consistently report increased confidence, sense of agency, critical perspective, and willingness and ability to speak out and act against discrimination. It has strengthened young women's leadership and confidence as citizens and political actors, inspiring them to educate, organize, and empower themselves and other young women to address problems together and challenge violence in every aspect of their lives. Finally, it has become a way to influence and inform the public, parents, schools, and local leaders, and hence change public discourse, attitudes, and behavior.

WHY IT WORKED

The girls' experience has shown that boxing can be a powerful tool for equipping girls and young women to protect themselves and ensure their security, and also to transform social relations of power that oppress, abuse, exploit, demean, or marginalize young people on the basis of their gender, age, ability, religion, location, class, tribe, or ethnicity. Through boxing, a safe space was created for young women to discuss and face their insecurities, including environmental degradation, violence at home and in the community, and the inability of the Kenyan government to support their basic needs.

continued on next page ›

KEY PRINCIPLES

MAKE THE PERSONAL POLITICAL

Boxing serves to politicize gender oppression by operating according to the feminist maxim "the personal is political." By fostering a safe space (*see: PRINCIPLE: Foster safer spaces*) for girls and women to share experiences and identify common challenges, participants begin to understand that their personal struggles are the consequences of an abusive and patriarchal social structure which they must work together to dismantle.

CREATE MANY POINTS OF ENTRY

In Nairobi, boxing is used as an entry point for discussing difficult topics related to sex and sexuality, as well as addressing issues related to violence against women. It's hard sometimes to directly confront controversial political issues, but when it is grounded in something as personal and physical as boxing, people have a greater chance of opening up. Sports have broad appeal, especially to youth; they seem non-political and less threatening. Boxgirls took those attractive qualities and provided a gateway to engage deeply in political issues that affected them.

KEY THEORY

FEMINISM

In her introduction to *Changing Their World: Concepts and Practices of Women's Movements* (Association of Women's Rights in Development [AWID], 2008), Srilatha Batliwala argues for an understanding of feminism as:

"an ideology and an analytical framework that is both broader and sharper than it was in the 60s and 70s . . . . We now stand not only for gender equality, but for the transformation of all social relations of power that oppress, exploit, or marginalize any set of people, women and men, on the basis of their gender, age, sexual orientation, ability, race, religion, nationality, location, class, caste, or ethnicity . . . . We seek a transformation that would create gender equality within an entirely new social order — one in which both men and women can individually and collectively live as human beings in societies built on social and economic equality, enjoy the full range of rights, live in harmony with the natural world, and are liberated from violence, conflict and militarization" (Batliwala 2008).

RELATED

O O O O

Feminism » *p. 184*

Public narrative (story of self, us, and now) » *p. 222*

LEARN MORE

The Fragile Strength | Patricia Esteve, 2015

Box Girl | Jackie Adiwinata, 2013

BoxGirls Kenya | FICCS Channel, 2012

Kenyan Boxgirl | BBC World Service, 2015

BURMESE STUDENTS' LONG MARCH

Myanmar | *November 2014-March 2015*

In 2014, hundreds of students embarked on a 360-mile-long march across Myanmar to protest the military-controlled Parliament's attempt to outlaw student unions.

Joseph Wah

In 2011, over 50 years of military rule in Myanmar (also known as Burma) formally ended and, under a new quasi-civilian government, the country opened up to the world. However, significant challenges remain. One of these challenges emerged in 2014 when the military-backed government introduced the National Education Law. Disguised as a so-called "reform" process, the law's true intent was to institute a new, oppressive education system. Under the law, existing student unions would be outlawed and replaced with state-sponsored (and controlled) student and teacher associations.

Student unions called for amendments to the draft law, but were ignored. Although small in number, the unions chose to stand up and fight back. The military-backed government was particularly anxious about student union protests, as students have a strong legacy of playing leading roles in major democracy movements in the past, ranging from the struggle for independence from colonial powers to the various movements against oppressive military regimes, including the 8888 uprising and the 2007 Saffron Revolution.

Dramatic confrontations between students and security forces, like the one captured in this Soe Zeya Tun image, helped the student movement to build support and attention, while putting pressure on the government to negotiate.

> *"Students have been at the center of democracy movements throughout Myanmar's history."*

The students' strategy was to recruit supporters, counter the proposed reforms, and push for better funding for education, all at the same time. Two months after the law was approved, students launched a four-day protest in Yangon and called on the parliament and government to open dialogue with them within 60 days to discuss amendments to the law.

As their calls for dialogue were ignored, students decided to launch a protest march from Mandalay to Yangon in January 2015 — a 360-mile march from central to lower Myanmar. The long march was a very strategic move for the students. It gave voice to the widespread discontent with the problematic law and its creation of state-sponsored student and teacher associations. Students held public rallies in dozens of major cities in the country, both separately and as part of the long march.

When the brave young students took to the street, public and civil society extended their support as they became much more aware of the undemocratic law, which had been approved without scrutiny. The long march allowed the public and media to take the time to understand flaws in the law as well as flaws in the education reform plan as a whole. The campaign gained momentum and occupied front pages of newspapers for months. Monks, youth, civil society, celebrities, and the general public were all supportive of the student protesters. As public support grew, it undermined any legitimacy the unpopular, newly formed, state-sponsored student association might have had. The public realized they were nothing more than an attempt to undermine the independent student unions.

WHY IT WORKED

Although the protest march was violently attacked by the government before it reached Yangon, and more than a hundred students and supporters were jailed, the four-month-long campaign did force representatives of parliament and government to dialogue with the students. This dialogue began a parliamentary discussion to amend the law, the results of which have yet to be seen. The campaign was also a massive inspiration to the Burmese people, as well as a politically useful reminder that the country, despite ongoing reform, is still under a repressive government. By renewing the struggle for genuine democracy in the new political landscape, student unions regained public recognition, and made a strong case for their ongoing leadership role.

WHY IT FAILED

Part way through the march, the government announced it would meet with the students to discuss amendments. But the students were determined to make it all the way to Yangon. They wanted to make a mark by completing the long march, even though the government threatened a violent crackdown if they continued to march past Letpadan, a town about 90 miles north of Yangon. They could have celebrated success without reaching Yangon, and thus avoided the crackdown. Now, most of the student leaders are facing trials, with few left to monitor the process of amending the education law to ensure the government keeps its promises.

continued on next page ›

KEY TACTIC

TREK

The tactical choice of a long march, or trek, was a smart one for several reasons. It was a bold and dramatic way to bring the students' cause to the people. By marching through many towns and villages, students engaged people across the country, not just in the largest city, Yangon. It also created a long campaign narrative, allowing the students to slowly build support and attention, as well as pressure on the government. Finally, in a sense, it also gave the government enough time to give in to the students' core demand.

KEY PRINCIPLES

MAINTAIN NONVIOLENT DISCIPLINE

Students have been at the center of democracy movements throughout Myanmar's history. To maintain that legacy and hold the high moral ground, as well as ensure the campaign received traditional support from the public, it was vital for the students on the long march to remain nonviolent.

LEAD WITH SYMPATHETIC CHARACTERS

Because of the heroic role Burmese students have historically played in their country's struggle for democracy, the Burmese people were already predisposed to see the students on the long march in a sympathetic light. So, once they witnessed the bravery of those who marched, and the violent response of the government, the public quickly got behind the students, and many high-profile supporters began speaking out for education reform.

KEY THEORY

DIRECT ACTION

When the new law outlawed existing student unions, students could have simply accepted the government's new rules. Instead, they took matters into their own hands. Not only did the unions refuse to comply with the law, they recruited more members and went on the offensive, strengthening their legitimacy by winning the sympathy and support of the people.

RELATED

Schools of Struggle » *p. 60*
Zapatista Caravan » *p. 100*

Civil disobedience » *p. 108*

Seek safety in support networks » *p. 150*

Al faza'a (a surge of solidarity) » *p. 172*

Spectrum of allies » *p. 232*

LEARN MORE

National Education Law – Student Protests | Burma Partnership, 2015

History Lessons | Bertil Lintner, The Irrawaddy, 2015

FLOWER SPEECH CAMPAIGN

Myanmar | 2014-present

In 2014, Burmese activists launched the Panzagar ("flower speech") campaign to counter hate speech in Myanmar in response to a rise in anti-Muslim violence.

Thinzar Shunlei Yi

In 2014, the Panzagar ("flower speech") campaign was launched to counter hate speech in Myanmar (also known as Burma) in response to a rise in anti-Muslim violence. *Al Jazeera* had reported 250 people killed in the violence, and more than 140,000 displaced and living in camps. The victims were predominantly from the minority Muslim Rohingya population, although some Buddhist monasteries, homes, and businesses were also burned down in revenge attacks. Flowers, the key image of the campaign, symbolize peace in Myanmar.

Although groups such as women and the lesbian, gay, bisexual, and transgender communities have also come under attacks online, the majority of the recent surge in hate speech has been aimed at Myanmar's Muslim community. According to a report from the Myanmar Centre for Responsible Business, almost 90 percent of all online hate speech it reviewed was aimed at the Muslim community.

The Panzagar campaign was initiated by Nay Phone Latt, youth leader, blogger, and member of regional parliament, who in 2008 had been sentenced to more than 20 years in prison for blogging about the 2007 Saffron Revolution, but who was released in 2012. The campaign aims to promote the responsible use of social media and raise awareness of the serious consequences of online behavior. The campaign partners with local young graphic designers and Facebook to create a set of positive "digital stickers" that users can share on the social media platform in response to any hate speech they encounter.

These stickers tend to depict, in animé style, a cute young woman with a flower in her mouth, using Buddhist imagery to symbolize a commitment not to use or tolerate speech that can spread hate among people. Within days, thousands of people had liked Panzagar's Facebook page, and many, including several public figures, have posted photographs of themselves holding flowers in their mouths. This is a courageous act in a country where anti-Muslim sentiment is growing and

"Flowers, the key image of the campaign, symbolize peace in Myanmar."

Flowers, which symbolize peace in Myanmar, became the key image of the Panzagar campaign against hate speech.

where there have been fatal clashes — most recently in July 2014 in Mandalay, after a false rumor that a Buddhist woman had been raped by Muslim men surfaced online and went viral on Facebook.

In September 2015, Facebook's community standards were translated into Burmese for the first time. The standards are sent to users mostly through promoted posts that Facebook hopes will lead users to think twice before they share content that could be deemed inflammatory towards marginalized groups.

The campaign has also gone beyond social media and into rural communities. The team has created a "Travelling Panzagar" project going to different states and regions to speak about the campaign and the importance of countering hate speech with "flower speech."

WHY IT WORKED

There are some great lessons to be learned from the #FlowerSpeech campaign. By combining an active presence on social media with public events, music, and stickers, the campaign makes it very easy for people to participate *(see: PRINCIPLE: Create many points of entry)*, and for passive supporters to become actively involved *(see: METHODOLOGY: Spectrum of allies p. 232)*. The campaign effectively countered hate speech among Buddhist extremists by invoking the Buddhist code of ethical conduct — in particular, the tenet of "right speech," or avoiding abusive, divisive, or harmful speech *(see: PRINCIPLE: Know your community)*. Finally, by condensing the campaign message into a simple, powerful, and culturally resonant image — people posing with the padauk flower, Myanmar's national flower, in their mouths — the campaign ensured that its message would be clearly and immediately understood by everyone who saw it *(see: THEORY: Memes)*.

WHY IT FAILED

Overall, #FlowerSpeech was widely adopted by youth all across Myanmar. One early criticism of the campaign, and a lesson for other activists, was around the choice of images in the early graphics: Some criticized the female images as overly sexualized, or too generically Asian and not Burmese-specific, or even overly stereotyped. Changes were made to reflect these criticisms. Another criticism noted that holding a flower in your mouth literally could prevent you from speaking, and that the campaign should not be understood as condoning silence in the face of hatred. It was also recognized that Panzagar was not a solution for all hate crimes, but rather a way to equip supporters with an easy way to respond to, and defuse, hate speech when they encountered it.

continued on next page ›

KEY PRINCIPLE

USE YOUR CULTURAL ASSETS

Holding a traditional flower in your mouth to symbolize the foundational Buddhist tenet of ethical conduct made the message familiar, accessible, and compelling to its target audience, as well as across other cultures.

KEY THEORY

ACTION LOGIC

Placing a flower (a traditional symbol of peace) in your mouth had a powerful effect — it was not only visually beautiful and evocative of the message, it also physically interfered with speaking hate speech.

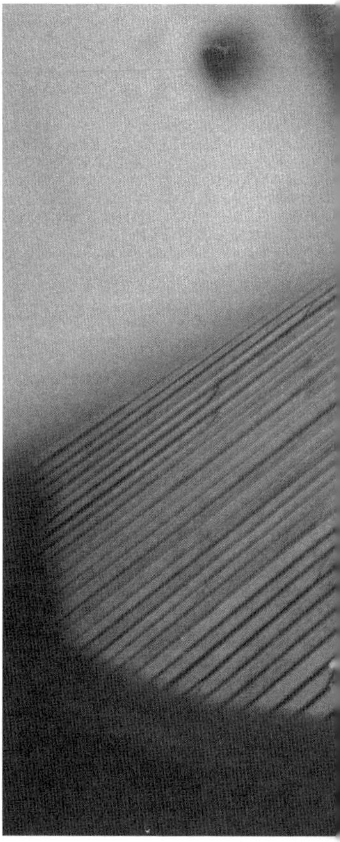

The Flower Speech campaign harnessed the sharing of selfies like this one, which consists of campaigners from different religions and ethnic groups, to counter the proliferation of hate speech online. Photo: Agence France-Presse

RELATED

Spectrum of allies » *p. 232*

LEARN MORE

Using "Flower Speech" and New Facebook Tools, Myanmar Fights Online Hate Speech
| Mari Michener Oye, The Washington Post, 2014

Hate Speech Pours Poison into the Heart
| San Yamin Aung, The Irrawaddy, 2014

HACKING APARTHEID

South Africa | 1980-1994

At the height of the anti-apartheid struggle, South African freedom fighters and hackers created an encrypted communication network that connected the leadership in exile with operatives in South Africa.

"Cryptography is the ultimate form of nonviolent direct action."
—Julian Assange

Sophie Toupin

During the apartheid era in South Africa, the ban imposed on the African National Congress (ANC) party meant that anti-apartheid activists were under constant surveillance, and were frequently forced into exile, arrested, jailed, tortured, or even killed.

Until the beginning of the 1980s, the ANC had a very limited communication network. It often used couriers who traveled in and out of the country to carry instructions, banned literature, and pamphlets. It also used Radio Freedom, the ANC's propaganda wing, to inform and inspire supporters. However, because communication methods were limited in their effectiveness, due in part to the distance separating ANC leaders in exile in Zambia from activists in South Africa, the creation of an encrypted communication system greatly improved the ANC's organizing capacities.

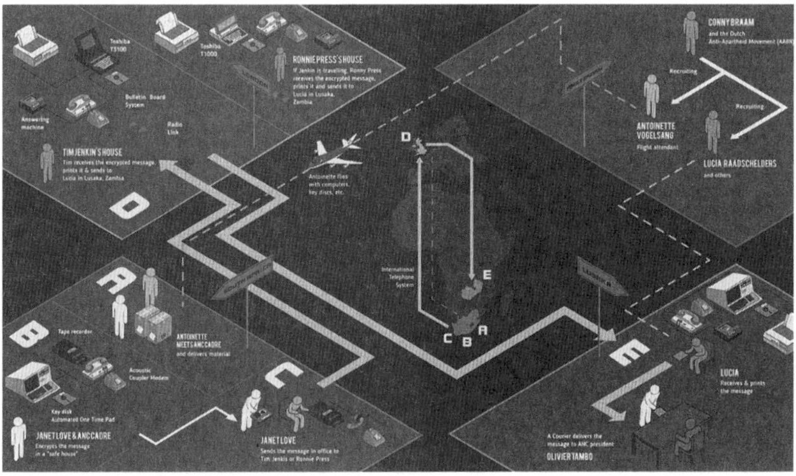

Infographic showing the African National Congress (ANC) communication network during apartheid. Infographic: Ariel Acevedo | CC BY-NC-SA

> *"The creation of an encrypted communication system greatly improved the ANC's organizing capacities."*

When exiled in London in the 1980s, the South African freedom fighter and hacker Tim Jenkin crafted an encrypted communication network that enabled operatives working underground in South Africa to report back to and communicate secretly with the African National Congress (ANC) leadership in exile in Zambia.

Known as Operation Vula, the system worked like this: Once it was fully up and running in 1988, Janet Love, a commander with Umkhonto weSizwe (MK), the armed wing of the ANC, would go to a safe house set up by a Canadian anti-apartheid couple and type a message on a laptop computer that had been smuggled in a few months before by Antoinette, a Dutch anti-apartheid flight attendant acting as a mule for the ANC. After typing the message and enciphering it, she would pass it out through the computer's serial port to an acoustic coupler modem. In this manner, she converted the digital data to sound, and the audio was recorded on a small cassette tape recorder. She would then dial Tim Jenkin in London, who had in his apartment a special answering machine attached to his landline phone to receive messages from South Africa. Jenkin played the received audio message back through a similar acoustic modem coupler attached to his computer, which converted it back to digital. The digital data would be deciphered using a matching floppy disk, which would make the plain text appear on Jenkin's computer screen. The floppy disk was based on an algorithm Jenkin had taken years to craft and polish. Depending on the content of the message, Jenkin would re-encipher it and pass it on to Lusaka, Zambia, where the senior leadership of the ANC was based. There, Lucia, another Dutch anti-apartheid activist, would receive Jenkin's enciphered message, decipher it, and print it out. A foot courier would pick up the message in Lucia's flat to take it to the senior ANC members.

By the late 1980s, the mass resistance in South Africa had reached unprecedented levels due to the fearless work of underground ANC activists, many of whom had slipped back into the country after having been exiled. The underground communication network became a highly effective means of passing information across borders to coordinate the anti-apartheid struggle. The anti-colonial hacking experimentation in the 1980s and 1990s came at a time when personal computers were just emerging, when cryptography was becoming recognized by many states as a weapon, and when countries such as the United States were restricting the selling of computers to South Africa for fear they would be used to strengthen the apartheid system.

Anti-apartheid activists were under constant surveillance, and were frequently forced into exile, arrested, jailed, tortured, or even killed. Here, workers leaving a May Day rally in Johannesburg in 1986 are questioned by armed police. Photo: Paul Weinberg

WHY IT WORKED

The encrypted communication network was successful for many reasons. First, it was on the cutting edge of an emerging technological practice and ethos: hacking. The hackers responsible worked relentlessly to develop their algorithm and perfect its use. Second, the number of people who knew about the system were few (about ten), lowering the chances for infiltration. Third, an extensive network of global anti-apartheid activists were raising awareness about the brutality of the regime, while at the same time lobbying their governments to apply diplomatic and economic pressure. Many also raised money for the larger movement. By itself, the encrypted communication system could not have brought about change, but in the context of a strong anti-apartheid movement acting on many fronts, it proved a powerful means for an outlawed organization to communicate and coordinate actions.

WHY IT FAILED

The development and use of encryption is essential for social movements to counter state, corporate, and other surveillance. However, encryption alone will not bring about social transformation. Hackers who are developing such tools must be connected to larger social movements, and social movements ought to become closer to the hacker community so each can learn from the other. Additionally, while developing and using encryption is no doubt important, community organizing in the open remains essential to transforming society for the better.

continued on next page ›

KEY TACTIC

ENCRYPTION

Encryption enabled the building of an underground communication system that not only established a strong international communication network among key figures of the anti-apartheid movement, but also limited the apartheid regime's ability to surveil. While for many encryption projects today encryption is an end in itself, Operation Vula provides an example of a more practical encryption project, aimed at a politically specific and highly context-dependent outcome. It was not only about safeguarding communications, it was about enabling the exchange of strategic and tactical information crucial to the ultimate aim of liberating a people from oppression.

KEY PRINCIPLE

PRACTICE DIGITAL SELF-DEFENSE

The development of a non-commercial encrypted communications infrastructure was indispensable to the anti-apartheid movement within and beyond South Africa, as it struggled against the surveillance, repression, and brutality of the apartheid regime. This network helped overcome a vicious circle: "Leaders could not go [to South Africa] because there were no underground structures in place to guarantee their safety; the underground structures could not develop because there were no key leaders in the country" (Jenkin, 1995).

RELATED

Seek safety in support networks » *p. 150*

Postcolonialism » *p. 196*
The Global South » *p. 188*

O O O O

KEY THEORY

HACKING

Hacking can be loosely defined as a practice that involves programming and/or tinkering with technology. Anthropologist Gabriella Coleman (2014) defines a hacker "as a technologist with a penchant for computing" and a hack as "a clever technical solution arrived at through non-obvious means." At the time, Jenkin did not identify as a hacker. Nevertheless, his tinkering with the phone system, computers, encryption, and acoustic coupler modems, among others, depended upon his ability to repurpose technologies through non-obvious means. It is perhaps unsurprising, then, that when asked if Jenkin considers himself a hacker today, he responded in the affirmative.

LEARN MORE

Talking to Vula: The Story of the Secret Underground Communications Network of Operation Vula | Tim Jenkin, 1995

The Vula Connection | YouTube, 2014

Escape from Pretoria | YouTube, 2013

Obfuscation: A User's Guide for Privacy and Protest | Finn Brunton and Helen Nissenbaum, MIT Press, 2015

HONK AT PARLIAMENT

Beirut, Lebanon | *June 2013*

In June 2013, citizens began honking their horns outside Lebanon's Parliament to tell MPs that their time in office had expired. The protest spread until they were honked at everywhere they went.

Hassan Tabikh

According to Lebanese Electoral Law No. 25/2008, the official mandate of an elected Parliament is four years. After one term is over, new elections must take place in line with civil and constitutional rights guaranteed for the people. Nonetheless, the 2009 Parliament, with a term set to expire in May 2013, voted to extend its mandate for a further 17 months.

On June 6, 2013, I and five other youths gathered in the crowded Abo Assaf cafe in the heart of the bustling Lebanese capital. We were dismayed by the Parliament's decision, and were determined to do something about it. We invited others, growing to a group of 15 that started brainstorming ideas for pressuring Parliament to call new elections. Many demonstrations had already occurred, but all had been repetitious, conventional, and ultimately ineffective.

We wanted results. We wanted something easy to participate in, yet flashy, nonviolent, and doable with zero budget. After many ideas were fleshed

"We learned that you do not need a lot of money to launch a strong and effective campaign. What it took was a bit of creativity and a lot of persistence."

out, someone said: "We must not allow them to stay in Parliament in a quiet atmosphere." This sparked ideas of noise disruptions, from music to whistling, until finally someone suggested the idea of honking horns, which the group eventually unanimously endorsed.

We tried it first using air horns. In groups of ones and twos, we entered the zone around the Parliament. Because groups are not allowed to enter together, some of us were waiting at coffee shops, restaurants, and hotels within the vicinity of the Parliament. The first horn took the policemen by surprise, and then the horns of 35 participants filled the air.

"No rule without popular legitimacy," reads a banner hanging on Beirut's Dawra Bridge in 2013.

"The horns were an obstacle," said one MP to a TV reporter as he emerged from a parliamentary session. "We were not able to hear each other." Our presence was impossible to ignore. We were interrupting business-as-usual. Our discontent and demands were being heard loud and clear.

We continued with the action on a weekly basis while Parliament was in session. Participant numbers increased dramatically until the police reacted by barring the public from the Parliament zone. In response, people began to honk from their balconies, in the streets, and from their cars wherever they spotted a car with the parliamentary insignia.

Our protest had started with 20 people with handheld air horns. Within three weeks, it had grown to thousands of people, using every kind of honking device imaginable. People were honking at MPs everywhere they went. Members of Parliament were visibly disturbed; some of them changed their license plates to hide their identity to avoid being honked at.

In spite of this widespread wave of protest, as well as all the media coverage and the nuisance caused to MPs, new elections have not yet been held. After the initial 17-month extension passed, the Parliament enacted another extension of its mandate for an additional 31 months, until June 2017.

Nonetheless, we created a new culture of protest in Lebanon: Now it is a tradition to honk at illegal parliamentarians whenever you've spotted one. With every honk, parliamentarians are reminded of what they know deep in their horn-battered bones: They are unlawful representatives of the public, effectively "occupying" the people's place.

This fight is not over. We will honk at them until they are gone.

WHY IT WORKED

The campaign worked because it was both creative and straightforward. The message was easy to grasp, and was already very topical in Lebanon. The tactic was simple and easy to join in on. Honking your horn was an inexpensive, fun, and emotionally satisfying way to express your disapproval at illegitimate authority figures.

We learned that it is important to believe in what you do, and that you are not alone in your struggle. We also learned that you do not need a lot of money to launch a strong and effective campaign. What it took was a bit of creativity and a lot of persistence.

WHY IT FAILED

We also learned that just because your idea catches fire, and you get a lot of people to join in, that does not always mean you will succeed. Lebanon is severely divided along political and religious lines, and in spite of general disgust at the illegal Parliament, people were under a lot of social pressure to support their sectarian affiliates in Parliament. People were also afraid of police repression. For both of these reasons, it was hard for the campaign to escalate enough to bring the sustained pressure it needed to succeed.

continued on next page ›

KEY TACTIC

NOISE-MAKING PROTEST (CACEROLAZO)

Lebanese people love music, whistling, honking, and clapping. Horns are usually used as a warning of danger, which made a strong statement about the illegal status of MPs. Noise-making objects, such as horns, are small, widely available, and easy to sneak through police checkpoints. They are disruptive yet nonviolent; they peacefully penetrated the walls and windows of the Parliament building, yet were loud enough to challenge its business-as-usual atmosphere.

KEY PRINCIPLE

SIMPLE RULES CAN HAVE GRAND RESULTS

Spot a parliamentarian? Honk! This was the simple formula that allowed the protest to spread quickly and widely. All that was needed was a horn, and knowing what to honk at: a Parliament license plate, the Parliament building, or the MPs themselves. This straightforward concept enabled large-scale public participation across different locations and times.

RELATED

Yellow Pigs in Parliament » p. 96

Would you like some structure with your momentum? » p. 166

Al faza'a (a surge of solidarity) » p. 172

Spectrum of allies » p. 232

O O O O

KEY THEORY

ALIENATION EFFECT

Before the honk protest began, MPs pretended to have a mandate; they were engaged in a pantomime play of democracy, which the public, as audience, passively participated in. If you passed an MP in the street or walked by the Parliament building, you could only be disgruntled by the fact that they had a false mandate. The honking campaign turned this banality into an outrage, making the familiar situation of non-representative government seem visibly odd, causing the MPs to feel out of place, and revealing to the audience (the Lebanese public) the hidden mechanisms of the play.

LEARN MORE

For the Republic | Youtube, 2013

For the Republic official page | Facebook

MINISKIRT MARCH

Harare, Zimbabwe | 2014

After a video circulated in 2014 showing the public abuse and harassment of a woman in Harare, Zimbabwe, women organized a miniskirt march to protest widespread street harassment and to push for safe spaces.

Angeline Makore

In Zimbabwe there is a cultural ideology that dictates that women are not allowed to wear revealing clothes, and if they do, men can publicly harass them with impunity. However, this ideology is now being challenged in the streets. In December 2014, social media in Zimbabwe and around the world lit up with a video showing a young woman being harassed and stripped naked at a taxi stand by rowdy men calling her all sorts of degrading names, allegedly because her dress was too short.

The video enraged the activist community, especially women's rights activists and human rights defenders. The women activists said "enough is enough," that it was high time they did something to challenge violence against women head-on. Various ideas for addressing the matter were put forward, but the one that stood out was dubbed a "miniskirt march."

The protest march was organized by Katswe Sistahood, a movement of dynamic young women fighting for women's sexual and reproductive health and rights in Zimbabwe, and publicized through word-of-mouth and the involvement of grassroots women's organizations. Scores of women showed up in miniskirts and tight-fitting clothes to parade through the streets of Harare, protesting against the harassment they encounter on a daily basis.

Although the march was received with mixed feelings from the general public, it played a pivotal role in Zimbabwe in addressing the violation of women's rights. The attackers who stripped the young woman were eventually arrested, remanded in prison, and are facing charges of indecent assault. The march also caught the attention of female political leaders like First Lady Grace Mugabe, who declared during the official launch of International Women's Day 2015 in Harare, "let us give our children the freedom to dress as they please."

Safety, security, and freedom of expression are fundamental if young women are to reach their fullest potential. The ball is in our court to rise creatively against sexual harassment of women at home and in public.

> *"The ball is in our court to rise creatively against sexual harassment of women in the home and in public."*

Scene from the Miniskirt March. Photo: iHarare

KEY TACTIC

MASS STREET ACTION

Large numbers of women marching through the streets in miniskirts sparked an important debate around the horrendous treatment of girls and women in public. By seeking safety in numbers, these women ensured their voices rang out loud and clear against street sexual harassment.

KEY PRINCIPLE

FOSTER SAFER SPACES

Humiliation is one of the most insidious forms of gender violence. In response, many activists are working to create safe spaces for women in their homes, in the community, and in the streets. Similar miniskirt marches have been carried out in various other African countries, including Kenya, Swaziland, Uganda, and Tunisia.
The success or failure of these campaigns has depended on various factors including the sociocultural background of particular communities, as well as the religious and political environments, but all have sought to foster safe spaces for women as a way to encourage them to speak out against public harassment.

RELATED

Stripping Power in Uganda » p. 84

Feminism » p. 184

O O O O

KEY THEORY

FEMINISM

In Zimbabwe, violence against women is rife. Young women in particular are vulnerable to human rights abuses including rape, domestic violence, and sexual harassment in the streets, especially at taxi stands. Women's frustration is understandable in the face of the widespread harassment they face, including arbitrary arrests at night, domestic violence, sexual abuse, and limits to freedom of movement. Young feminist organizers are drawing on a long tradition of feminist thought and tactics as they grapple with how to stop this cycle of abuse and harassment. Miniskirt march participants marched under the banner of feminism, inspired by the movement's historic commitment to advancing women's equality and defending every woman's right to freedom of expression and movement.

WHY IT WORKED

The march succeeded because it seized upon a "moment of shame" and turned it into a moment of pride and power. The original woman's harassment at the taxi stand was unfortunately nothing new, except that it ended up on video and captured the nation's attention, providing a perfect organizing opportunity. By marching in the street, 200-strong, and not only shouting, "We can dress as we please," but also actually dressing as they pleased, these women transformed themselves from victims into survivors, turning their fear and isolation into power and togetherness. Maybe even more importantly, they turned the shame and blame put on them into pride and freedom. They flipped the script, doing the exact thing they'd always been told not to do, but doing it together, as an act of defiance.

LEARN MORE

Humiliation: The Latest Form of Gender Violence
| Sally Nyakanyanga, Africa Renewal, 2015

REPLACING COPS WITH MIMES

Bogotá, Colombia | *1995*

Faced with a notoriously corrupt traffic police force, many traffic deaths, and chaos on the roads, Bogotá mayor Antanas Mockus disbanded the corrupt cops and offered to retrain and rehire them . . . as mimes.

Tomaz Capobianco

In the early 1990s, Bogotá was a city in crisis. Poverty, corruption, and crime were endemic, public faith in government had bottomed out, and life in the capital had, for many, descended into a battle of all against all. This was the situation that philosophy professor Antanas Mockus stepped into when he was elected mayor — an unlikely politician with unconventional methods (he'd campaigned in a spandex superhero costume) and an uncommonly large mandate for radical political change.

In his two terms as mayor (1995-1997 and 2001-2003), Mockus catalyzed tremendous improvements to Bogotá. Launching civic campaigns that involved massive, voluntary public participation, the homicide rate fell 70 percent, while the percentage of homes with drinking water increased from 79 to 100 percent.

There is no better example of the mayor's audacious and highly effective approach than his program addressing traffic safety, which saw traffic fatalities drop by over 50 percent. After piloting the project with theater students, Mockus fired 3,200 traffic cops from a notoriously corrupt police force and then offered them the option to be retrained and hired back — as mimes. Four hundred accepted the offer, trading their handcuffs and batons for white gloves and face paint.

Each day, the mimes moved through traffic and seized on opportunities to dramatize the struggles and frustrations of drivers and pedestrians. They heaped scorn on cars blocking pedestrian crosswalks and then gestured as if repainting the crosswalk, endorsing its existence. They helped elderly people cross the street, and pretended to push cars blocking intersections out of the way. In addition to the mimes, Mockus also distributed 350,000 "thumbs-up/thumbs-down" cards that

"The mimes infused Bogotá's streets with common sense — or, rather, a sense of the commons."

In a Venezuelan initiative inspired by Bogotá, traffic cop mimes help shift social norms by dramatizing the struggles of pedestrians. Photo: Francisco Lizarazo

citizens could use to peacefully express approval or disapproval of others' traffic behavior.

At first glance, it seemed an absurd way to make traffic safer, and Mockus was ridiculed in the press for pursuing it. But gradually, by making fun of drivers and pedestrians who didn't follow basic rules and celebrating those who did, the mimes managed to transform the entire traffic culture of the city, successfully infusing Bogotá's streets with common sense — or, rather, a sense of the commons.

The construction of the urban environment, a duty usually reserved for engineers, architects, developers, and the like, became, under Mockus' mayorship, the responsibility of all urban inhabitants. His programs for Bogotá viewed citizens as political beings who are always already participating in the construction of their city, either with their good or bad attitudes.

"The mayor's genius," suggests Raymond Fisman, "was in recognizing that writing harsher laws or hiring more gun-toting policemen would be futile when confronted with a law-breaking culture. Instead he enabled Bogotá's citizens to make change themselves." Or as Mockus himself explains it, "Knowledge empowers people. If people know the rules and are sensitized by art, humor, and creativity, they are much more likely to accept change." Mockus proved that creativity and humor can work where legal punishment has failed.

Photo: Francisco Lizarazo

WHY IT WORKED

Mockus' program succeeded in changing the behavior of hundreds of thousands of individuals because it encouraged citizens to hold one another accountable. It directly challenged a culture of impunity, promoting instead a culture of shared responsibility for the urban environment. Instead of using traditional top-down procedures, Mockus created a program that required active participation of the public. As citizens saw that they could shape their own environment for the better, they developed a sense of pride and collective ownership.

continued on next page ›

KEY PRINCIPLES

USE STATE POWER TO BUILD PEOPLE POWER

Like so many other politicians who get swept into office with a mandate for radical reform, Mockus could have just settled into business as usual. But he didn't; instead he used his power to do something audacious. He didn't just "disarm" the traffic police, a wing of the repressive state apparatus he inherited (which would have been a stunning accomplishment in itself), he reinvented it, flipped it on its head. By turning corrupt state agents into gentle, beguiling civil servants, he created a "constructive vacuum" of state power that gave rise to people power. The lesson: The state won't "wither away" on its own, it must be creatively dismantled in a way that invites civil society to take responsibility for the self-regulation of society. Mockus understood this and took provocative action to move that vision forward.

KILL THEM WITH KINDNESS

Unlike the cops, who depend on coercive force, the mimes' only power was their capacity to scold or induce laughter. Because of their lack of authority and their vulnerability amidst the traffic, the mimes stood on the same level as other citizens, and thus were able to affect them more powerfully. It was precisely this empathic common ground that allowed the mimes to shift the traffic culture of Bogotá.

KEY THEORY

THE SOCIAL CURE

Part of the genius of the mayor's program was how it leveraged peer pressure to shift Bogotá's traffic from a culture of impunity to a culture of courtesy rooted in unspoken rules. The mimes set a new tone, but it was when motorists themselves took up the dramatization of these rules — through "thumbs-up/thumbs-down" cards and other devices — that a new sense of right and wrong, "cool" and "uncool," was established, changing social behavior across the board.

RELATED

Shame the authorities by doing their job » p. 154
Use humor to undermine authority » p. 160

LEARN MORE

Academic Turns City into a Social Experiment | Maria Cristina Caballero, Harvard Gazette, 2004

Bogotá Change | 2009

Antanas Mockus: Colombians Fear Ridicule More Than Being Fined | Sarah Marsh, The Guardian, 2013

Cards Against Harassment: Another Example of the Social Cure at Work

SCHOOLS OF STRUGGLE

São Paulo, Brazil | 2015-2016

Students occupied over 200 schools in São Paulo, Brazil to protest the governor's plan to close schools, forcing him to reverse course and igniting a wave of student resistance across the country.

Carolina Munis and Marcel Taminato

In September 2015, the governor of São Paulo, the richest state in Brazil, announced a so-called "reorganization" of public schools that concentrated students in fewer, larger schools in order to cut costs. The measure would have led to the closing of 94 institutions and the transfer of 311,000 students and more than 74,000 teachers, many of whom would have been relocated to schools far from their homes. The decision was made without any prior consultation with teachers, students, or families. And, even worse, the plan did not address any of the severe issues faced by the public education system, such as lack of teachers, lack of safety, overcrowded classrooms, crumbling infrastructure, and poor-quality meals — on the contrary, it only aggravated these issues.

In response to the announced plan, after street protests and appeals to the Secretary of Education, city councillors, and regional directors of education were

Students from the Maria José State School wrapped in traffic tape to represent being immobilized and silenced by the government. Photo: Arianne Vitale Cardoso

> *"The occupations soon became the educational spaces that the students had always wanted."*

met with silence, the students of Diadema State School decided to occupy their school, located on the outskirts of the state capital. The next day, students from Fernão Dias Paes State School, located in downtown São Paulo, did the same.

The state government made several attempts to intimidate and demobilize the students. They ordered that both schools be cleared, a decision that was soon overruled by a state court upholding the students' right to protest. State police were constantly showing up at the occupations, threatening the protesters and causing disruption. And the authorities fueled a media campaign to portray the students as vandals who were destroying and looting school property.

However, the repression only increased public support for the students: Their families and teachers, demonstrating their support, were quickly joined by artists, journalists, opinion makers, trade unions, social movements, and other groups.

The public outrage generated by the government and police attacks triggered a massive wave of school occupations: In the following weeks, 213 schools across the state were occupied by students opposing the "reorganization" plan.

The occupations soon became the educational spaces the students had always wanted *(see: THEORY: Prefiguration)*. There was a busy schedule of daily activities such as lectures, debates, public classes, and workshops on a variety of subjects (e.g. gender issues, direct democracy, digital culture, environmental education, permaculture, drugs and harm reduction, languages, etc.), most of which were crowdsourced to volunteers. Moreover, the students made sure that basic tasks such as cooking, cleaning, and safety were collective and self-organized. The collaborative and autonomous experience constituted a clear opposition to the government's authoritarian discourse of austerity, and was a practical display of the quality that the public education system had failed to provide. As the occupations grew, there was no indication that the status quo would prevail over a self-organized, autonomous student movement that had turned the ideal of free and democratic education into reality.

In December, after two months of occupations, the state government finally announced the suspension of the school reorganization plan. The next day, the Secretary of Education resigned. The students' uprising had launched a debate on the role of democracy in schools and the true meaning of public education. The students and their supporters emerged as a strong coalition with the ability to respond quickly to future attacks on education. And best of all, the movement soon spread beyond the state: In the following months, occupations took place in several other states in Brazil, reaching over 250 other schools in protest against precarious infrastructure, inferior meals, lack of quality, lack of transparency, and privatization of education, as well as demanding free public transportation.

WHY IT WORKED

Throughout the occupations, the students stayed on message and made sure their demand was clear: to end the reorganization plan enforced by the state government. Due to their ability to build a cohesive narrative stemming from a specific problem and offer clear paths to overcome this reality *(see: PRINCIPLE: The price of a successful attack is a constructive alternative)*, the high school students suddenly emerged as a powerful force in the struggle for free and quality public education across Brazil. Furthermore, students used the reorganization issue as a wedge to address other structural problems faced by the public education system, such as the poor wages and working conditions for teachers, the attacks from a neoliberal agenda backed by corporations, the lack of democratic practices, and decaying infrastructure.

Photo: Arianne Vitale Cardoso

continued on next page ›

KEY TACTIC

OCCUPATION

The occupations were initially intended to defend the schools against closing, but they also ended up serving as hubs to activate a solidarity network around the students' uprising. Almost every aspect of the daily life in the occupations was crowdsourced, from basic necessities such as food and materials, to the workshops and classes. Therefore, the tactic in itself served as a way to broaden the movement and build support.

KEY PRINCIPLES

BREAKFAST IS PERSUASIVE

The students used the occupation to create the schools they wanted. They built a fabulous schedule of classes, demonstrating that the claim that the students did not care about their studies was fallacious. While the government was calling them vandals, they were fixing what was broken with the voluntary help of the community.

CHOOSE TACTICS THAT SUPPORT YOUR STRATEGY

The occupation was not the only tactic employed by the students. In order to build up even more pressure, they made use of other actions simultaneously, such as street blockades in major avenues in São Paulo, music festivals with the support of famous singers, mass demonstrations, and creative interventions.

USE YOUR CULTURAL ASSETS

The students created and recorded songs, many of which were political adaptations of widely popular Brazilian funk songs. These interventions were boosted by nimble and impactful communications on social media, independent media, and the use of celebrities, which served as a reliable alternative to the conservative mainstream press. Updates on each of the occupations were posted on an hourly basis, and a channel was established to connect with supporters and issue calls to action.

O O O O

KEY THEORY

ACTION LOGIC

When the students demonstrated that quality public education could be effectively implemented with no financial or political excuses, it was easy for the public to understand what was going on: Students were keeping schools open in order to keep schools open.

LEARN MORE

Wave of High School Occupations Across São Paulo | Left Voice, 2015

RELATED

⅄ II O ⌐

Burmese Students' Long March » p. 26

Zapatista Caravan » p. 100

⅄ ⅄ ⅄ ⅄

Civil disobedience » p. 108

II II II II

Seek safety in support networks » p. 150

Shame the authorities by doing their job » p. 154

Would you like some structure with your momentum? » p. 166

O O O O

Neoliberalism » p. 192

⌐ ⌐ ⌐ ⌐

Pillars of power » p. 210

Power mapping » p. 216

SMART objectives » p. 226

The onion tool » p. 238

SIGN LANGUAGE SIT-IN

Harare, Zimbabwe | 2012

Deaf activists in Zimbabwe stood up (and sat-in) to demand access to information in sign language, successfully pressuring the national broadcaster to include sign language interpretation in news broadcasts.

Agness Chindimba

When people in Zimbabwe talk about disability, the main assumption is that disability is synonymous with physical impairments. Deafness is often overlooked because it is not visible at first glance. As a result, deaf people tend to lag behind and live at the periphery of society. Their marginalization is compounded by a general lack of access to information, including the Zimbabwe Broadcasting Corporation (ZBC)'s failure to provide information to the deaf community. However, beginning in 2012, in a remarkable campaign targeting the ZBC, deaf people mobilized themselves and their allies, stood up, claimed their constitutional right to information, and demanded that their voices be heard.

First, a delegation was sent to the Disability Advisor in the President's Office to advocate for the needs of the deaf community in Zimbabwe, after which he wrote a supportive letter to the Ministry of Information and Publicity, airing the concerns that he had received from the delegation. Next, they visited the ministry to deliver the Disability Advisor's letter, but to their surprise, the secretary advised them to make a phone call to place an appointment! They responded that they could not make a phone call because they are deaf, and they did not have the minister's cell phone number so could not send a text message.

Unwilling to leave empty-handed, the delegation opted to sit in and wait for the minister to come out of his office. Eventually, they were given 20 minutes to discuss their concerns with the minister, after which he provided a supportive letter to hand over to ZBC.

Now armed with two letters of support, the delegates made clear to the ZBC that if their grievances were ignored, they would refuse to pay television licences, and mobilize other deaf people in Zimbabwe to join the campaign. The broadcasting representatives promised to offer them a slot during the day to air a program in sign language. The delegates responded that deaf people in Zimbabwe worked during the day, just like everyone else. They demanded prime time access, and were soon granted it.

This campaign by deaf people in Zimbabwe saw the introduction of sign language on all ZBC weekday news bulletins. Prior to this, sign language was only offered during the lunch hour news bulletin. The activists also won 30 minutes

"The deaf community did not lose heart when they met challenges such as lack of response from authorities, nor did they take 'no' for an answer."

The Zimbabwean sign language alphabet, demonstrated by Belinda Ndlovu.

of airtime each week for a program in sign language disseminating information of interest to deaf people. Thus was born Action Power, a program that airs on national television every Tuesday evening, raising awareness about deaf culture and sign language, and providing information to the deaf community on a variety of topics. Other producers for programs aired on ZBC have started to emulate Action Power by hiring interpreters for their programs.

Buoyed by these victories, the deaf community set its sights on further progress: They feel the national broadcaster should pay them for their productions (currently ZBC gets them for free). Also, there is still a need for sign language during weekend news bulletins and current affairs programming, as well as captioning for soaps and dramas. The battle was won but the war would continue.

WHY IT WORKED

The protest by the deaf community was successful because of their unity and persistence. Participants were willing to pursue common goals and speak with one voice despite the fact that they came from different organizations and political and socio-economic backgrounds. They put their differences aside and worked hand in hand to demand their rights. The deaf community did not lose heart when they met challenges such as lack of response from authorities, nor did they take “no” for an answer.

continued on next page ›

KEY TACTIC

OCCUPATION

Sitting in at the office of the Minister of Information and Publicity and refusing to leave the building without seeing the Minister proved an effective tactic for pressuring him to meet with the delegation and act on its demands.

KEY PRINCIPLE

CHOOSE YOUR TARGET WISELY

Though the primary target of this campaign was the Zimbabwe Broadcasting Corporation, organizers recognized that the real power lay with the Minister of Information and Publicity, so that is where they focused their pressure. Without that supportive letter from the Disability Advisor in the President's Office, direct appeals to the ZBC likely would have required far greater levels of mobilization to be effective.

RELATED

Civil disobedience » *p. 108*

Power mapping » *p. 216*
SMART objectives » *p. 226*

KEY THEORY

SOCIAL MODEL OF DISABILITY

The campaign was underpinned by the belief in the social model of disability. The model acknowledges that the problem of disability does not reside in the individual, nor does it lie in the impairment, but in the response of the society towards a person with a disability. For deaf people, the major barriers have to do with attitudes and communication, resulting in exclusion from participation in mainstream society, poor services, and violation of rights, especially the right to access to information. This campaign sought to directly challenge these attitudes by dramatizing the deaf community's need for access to information.

LEARN MORE

ZBC-TV Saluted by the Deaf for Complying with the New Constitution | Deaf Zimbabwe Trust, 2015

STOLEN GAS CAMPAIGN

Jordan | 2014-present

Grassroots Jordanian activists mobilized popular opposition against a $15 billion deal with Israel to import natural gas, both before and after the deal was signed.

Samar Saeed

In September 2014, the Jordanian National Electric Power Company signed a letter of intent to import natural gas from the Israeli-controlled Leviathan fields, located offshore in Mediterranean waters. When news of the agreement broke, a massive grassroots campaign arose to oppose the deal, and when the deal was signed two years later, opposition grew ever stronger.

In the first few month of the campaign, a national coalition operating under the name "The Jordanian National Coalition Against Importing Gas from Israel," consisting of dozens of major political parties, trade unions, grassroots groups, parliamentarians, and others, was formed to consolidate broad yet unified public rejection of the deal *(see: PRINCIPLE: If you're not uncomfortable, your coalition is too small).*

The widespread anger was provoked by the fact that not only would this deal undermine the global efforts of the Boycott, Divestment, and Sanctions movement to isolate Israel for its violations against the Palestinian indigenous population, but would also threaten Jordan's economic stability and political sovereignty *(see: THEORY: Hamoq and hamas).*

On September 30, 2016, thousands of Jordanians marched to protest against the gas deal and call for its nullification. Photo: Yousef Al Gazawi

> *"Once the battle lines were drawn, very few people wanted to be seen as siding with the villains."*

The Jordanian regime hoped that the deal would normalize relations with a settler-colonial state and transform its "cold" peace with Israel into a warmer one. In contradiction to the regime's intentions, however, the deal provoked large numbers of people who had not been engaged in politics to become active organizers against it *(see: METHODOLOGY: Spectrum of allies p. 232)*.

The significance of this campaign, which continues to be waged even after the government signed the deal in September 2016, lies in the fact that it represents the longest and most widespread opposition movement in Jordan since the 2011 popular protests during the Arab Spring. The difference is that artivism has played a crucial role in manifesting opposition to the deal *(see: THEORY: Artivism)*. For examples, several video clips *(see: TACTIC: Music video p. 124)* and songs have been produced denouncing the government's decision. In a truly grassroots tactic of switching off the lights for an hour every Sunday night, artists, comedians, and musicians have performed in candlelight week after week to express their opposition.

Amongst the several active groups in this campaign was the Jordanian chapter of the Boycott, Divestment, and Sanctions (BDS) movement. One of the tactics that

Jordan BDS used was phone banking sessions to mobilize members of parliament *(see: TACTIC: Phone banking)*. When the tactic was first used in 2014, it was a huge success that led to forming a broad Parliamentary opposition that voted overwhelmingly not only against the deal but for cancelling the letter of intent. However, the reuse of this tactic in 2016 was not as fruitful, given that a higher vote threshold, and therefore more public pressure on the members of parliament, was required to challenge the government on a binding deal rather than a letter of intent *(see: PRINCIPLE: Don't fall in love with your tactics)*. The campaign continues at the time of writing, with more innovative ideas and escalatory tactics mushrooming every day *(see: PRINCIPLE: Escalate strategically)*.

WHY IT WORKED

The key to success has been activists' ability to galvanize public opinion against the deal by engaging various sectors of Jordanian society. The campaign effectively lobbied the Parliament, turning many MPs from supporters of the gas deal into opponents. Furthermore, the national coalition was sustained despite bumpy roads, and weekly popular action is still taking place in spite of increasing government repression. Do not underestimate what people's power and wit can achieve. The government was surprised by the power and unity of the people, and they were also embarrassed by the people's ability to scientifically negate their justifications.

WHY IT FAILED

The government eventually turned a blind eye to the people's will and the parliamentary vote, and went ahead with the deal— effectively waiting out the deal's opponents. The length of the campaign diffused people's anger after the initial, extremely broad-based, surge of support *(see: THEORY: Al faza'a [a surge of solidarity] p. 172)*, as many people were not committed to long-term organizing against it. The breadth of resistance and effective use of strategic escalation delayed the deal by two years, yet the escalation ultimately was not enough to dissuade the government from pushing through the deal.

continued on next page ›

KEY TACTIC

PHONE BANKING

Jordanian parliament and elections are not models of democracy: It was highly unusual for large numbers of people to call members of parliament to lobby them on an issue. This novelty made the tactic very effective. Probably for the first time, Jordanian members of parliament were having to defend their position, again and again, to members of the public. At the beginning, it was hard for MPs to believe that the activists calling them were not journalists, but later the phone banking tactic became the major political topic of the season and helped to build strong ties with parliamentarians, some of whom became strong allies of the campaign.

KEY PRINCIPLES

ESCALATE STRATEGICALLY

The campaign did not play all its cards at the beginning, as we were aware that we faced a long-term battle. Thus, the campaign began with awareness-raising and challenging government misinformation, expanded to demonstrations and petitions, then to mobilizing the majority of the parliament to vote against the deal and holding a people's trial against the government. This strategic escalation allowed the campaign to remain sustainable while ensuring that the government and the Jordanian National Electric Power Company continuously felt the heat of the opposition. The bigger the actions and the more ambitious the tactics, the greater the impact they had on the government's position.

PERSONALIZE AND POLARIZE

The first thing that campaigners and various groups did was to label the government and the National Electric Power Company as the villains for misleading the public by disseminating false information, and for jeopardizing the sovereignty and independence of the nation. As this framing of the issue became more and more popular, activists were able to persuade the general public to take sides. Once the battle lines were drawn, very few people wanted to be seen as siding with the villains.

O O O O

KEY THEORY

AL FAZA'A (A SURGE OF SOLIDARITY)

In a state of imminent threat or danger, people will put aside their differences and come together in large numbers to respond to an emergency. When the letter of intent was signed, people expected that a full deal would be reached within a few months, so tremendous numbers of people came forward to mobilize against it. After the threat faded, far fewer people remained part of the day-to-day organizing against the deal.

RELATED

Stop Prawer Plan » p. 78
Welcome to Palestine » p. 90

Music video » p. 124

Al faza'a (a surge of solidarity) » p. 172

Pillars of power » p. 210
Spectrum of allies » p. 232

LEARN MORE

Pumping Revenue Into Israel's Coffers: The Israeli-Jordan Gas Deal | Platform Research Center, 2014

#AgainstStolenGas Factsheet | Jordan BDS, 2014

STOP PRAWER PLAN

Palestine | 2013

In response to a draft Israeli bill that aimed to expel 70,000 Palestinian Bedouins from their ancestral land, Palestinians organized a massive campaign that led to the withdrawal of the proposed bill.

Nisreen Haj Ahmad

Official Israeli policy does not recognize the rights of the Palestinian Bedouins in the Negev to their ancestral land, and therefore prohibits them from accessing infrastructural services. Israel continually attempts to confiscate the land and destroy the homes and villages of the Bedouins as a means of slow yet systematic ethnic cleansing. The Prawer-Begin draft bill aimed to destroy 35 villages, making up 300 square miles of Bedouin land, and ethnically cleanse 70,000 Palestinians in one go. It was claimed that they had received the approval of the Bedouins on the plan.

With a four-vote majority, the bill passed in the Knesset (Israel's national legislature) on its first reading in June 2013. With such a large-scale plan of ethnic cleansing, this was seen as yet another Nakba (the Palestinian catastrophe of 1948). The goal of the Stop Prawer Plan campaign was to stop the Prawer draft from passing in its second and third readings. The bigger objective, of course, was to stop home demolitions and land expropriation of the Palestinians in the Negev, and to see their villages provided with infrastructure and services.

Initially, various actions were taken by local groups and political parties, yet the number of people mobilized was low. Disappointed by the number of participants, a group of young Palestinian Bedouins organized a campaign to ensure that the Prawer plan would not pass.

The campaign collected Bedouin signatures on the petition denouncing the law, organized a general strike on the day the Knesset committee visited the Negev, and, in alliance with other groups, lobbied the Knesset members to vote against the bill. The campaign organized a global Day of Rage *(see: TACTIC: Distributed action)* with actions in 34 cities around the world and across historic Palestine,

> *"Unlike what happens in many other campaigns, the campaign leaders spent most of their time organizing rather than mobilizing."*

Demonstrators in Haifa under attack by the Israeli police on the Day of Rage against the Prawer plan. The Israeli police used horses, water canons, and shock grenades to disperse the demonstrators. Dozens of protesters were arrested and several injured. Photo: Activestills

including in the Negev, Haifa, Yaffa, Jerusalem, Nablus, and Gaza. All these actions were accompanied by strong media outreach and coverage.

In parallel, all these peaceful actions were met by a violent crackdown by the Israeli police and army to repress Palestinians from nonviolently resisting their continued ethnic cleansing and forced expulsion from their ancestral lands. During the campaign, Israeli intelligence investigated dozens of campaigners and arrested many more who participated in peaceful demonstrations.

Despite the challenges, on the eve of the Day of Rage, the head of the Labor Party withdrew his support for the draft law. A week later the government decided to shelve it. The Palestinians won. Prawer did not pass.

WHY IT WORKED

Unlike what happens in many other campaigns, the campaign leaders spent most of their time organizing rather than mobilizing. To begin, they invested time in establishing, coordinating, and maintaining four teams, in addition to their core team: media, Israeli voices, international action, and Bedouin towns. This approach not only gave space for new leadership to develop, but also gave organizers the ability to sustain and escalate their efforts without depending solely on the core team.

continued on next page ›

⅄ ⅄ ⅄ ⅄

KEY TACTIC

DISTRIBUTED ACTION

In coordination with the Boycott, Divestment, and Sanctions movement, the organizers of the Stop Prawer Plan campaign were able to send a call to action to groups and organizations all over the world. Accessing this already-existing network of organized groups made action possible in 34 cities worldwide on the Day of Rage. As interest spread, groups they'd never even heard of contacted them and joined the day of action. This access and networking made all the difference.

II II II II

KEY PRINCIPLE

KNOW YOUR COMMUNITY

Initially, the collection of signatures on the petition refusing the Prawer Law was slow and tedious, given the distances involved. Municipal council elections were set for October 22, 2013, so the organizers smartly used these high-traffic points to collect signatures outside the polling stations and saw numbers on the petition multiply.

RELATED

Stolen Gas Campaign » p. 72

Civil disobedience » p. 108

Activate international mechanisms » p. 138
Would you like some structure with your momentum? » p. 166

Al faza'a (a surge of solidarity) » p. 172

Pillars of power » p. 210
Power mapping » p. 216
Spectrum of allies » p. 232

KEY THEORY

ACTION LOGIC

As action on the campaign was building, the Knesset committee tasked with studying the draft law decided to visit the Negev and meet with the heads of the Bedouin tribes to prove that the Bedouins approved the draft bill. The campaign leaders, along with other organizations, called for a general strike and took to the streets as the Knesset committee arrived. This way, even if the committee had found a few tribesmen to say they supported the bill, bigger numbers taking to the streets against the proposed law would speak far louder.

KEY METHODOLOGY

THEORY OF CHANGE

Because of limited time and resources, it was necessary for activists to choose their actions strategically and invest their limited resources smartly. Despite the many creative ideas that came up, the leaders decided to focus on a few assumptions, which became the guiding principles of their action and alliances. Their four theories of change were that the draft would not pass if: (1) Bedouins demonstrated in an organized way that they were against the draft law contrary to what Prawer said, (2) large numbers of people could be convinced to boycott Israel for being a racist and apartheid state, (3) Knesset members were pressured by their own constituencies, and (4) Israel's ability to secure order in the streets was jeopardized. Organizers recognized that only if one or more of these four conditions were realized would their opposition be taken seriously.

LEARN MORE

Demolition and Eviction of Bedouin Citizens of Israel in the Naqab (Negev) - The Prawer Plan | Adalah

Palestinian Civil Society Calls for Escalating BDS to Stop Israel's Racist Prawer Plan, Urges Inter-Parliamentary Union to Suspend Knesset's Membership | BDS movement, 2013

Forty-Thousand Bedouin Are Being Kicked Off Their Land by Israel | Vice, 2013

STRIPPING POWER IN UGANDA

Apaa Village, Uganda | 2015

Female elders in northern Uganda invoked powerful cultural taboos by removing their clothes in front of two government ministers who were attempting to grab their land, successfully chasing them away.

Phil Wilmot

For a number of years, a land conflict has been raging between residents of the oil-rich, fertile rural area of Amuru District in northern Uganda and the self-interested dictatorship and its corporate affiliates who were seeking to sell off the land. Several lives had been lost at the hands of abusive government agencies seeking to drive off those living on the land. In April 2015, the situation came to a head: The government began evicting people in Apaa Village by force, at night. They used the Uganda Wildlife Authority and the Uganda People's Defense Force (UPDF), setting homes and gardens on fire and physically attacking locals. This particular area had been sold by the adjacent district, as if that district (Adjumani) were the owner of

Members of Parliament, visibly upset by the bold display of nudity with which they are confronted, confer with the regional police commander at the roadblock in Apaa village. Photo: Sam Lawino, Acholi Times

"The Minister of Lands burst into tears at the sight."

land outside of its geographic reach. The buyer was a South African investor by the name of Bruce Martin, who wanted the land, which includes an animal reserve, for elite sports game hunting.

In response, community leaders working with organizers from Solidarity Uganda called for peaceful demonstrations. After trainings in nonviolent direct action, a few days of simple marches, and other related peaceful demonstrations, residents prepared to risk their lives, as more and more military personnel began setting up camp sites. Two government ministers, the Minister of Lands and the Minister of Internal Affairs (who is also a military general), came to demarcate land once and for all in an attempt to redistrict Apaa out of Amuru District and into Adjumani District.

To block the ministerial convoy, the community put up a roadblock in a forested area of the village *(see: TACTIC: Blockade)*. Local women stripped naked at the roadblock, invoking a powerful cultural omen or curse in Uganda, where it provokes deep shame to see a woman the age of one's mother naked. The Minister of Lands burst into tears at the sight and began begging the community to end the protest, trying to argue that he hadn't come to steal their land after all. The Minister of Internal Affairs attempted to dodge the situation altogether by looking away, but the massive number of people and the overwhelming sight of the elders flailing their naked limbs about prevented him from proceeding with his mission. The convoy returned to the capital city having failed to place the mark stones they had brought for redistricting.

Shortly thereafter, the military occupation in Apaa was disbanded. Many soldiers repented of their wrongdoings, claiming that they hated carrying out the orders of their superiors. Civil society groups organized local leaders to pass several resolutions, demanding the release of a few community leaders arrested in conjunction with the action, and insisting that the land of Apaa never be considered part of Adjumani District.

WHY IT WORKED

The action successfully used cultural omens and curses, which are embedded in the East African context as a tactic of cultural resistance, to stop the government from evicting people from their land *(see: PRINCIPLE: Use your cultural assets)*. Significantly, there were also hundreds, even thousands, of local residents prepared to defend the land from theft, but the first line of protection (naked female elders) was highly effective at shaming the ministers and chasing them away. The unexpected behavior from female elders attracted a lot of national and international media coverage, helping put land conflicts in northern Uganda in the spotlight *(see: PRINCIPLE: Seek safety in support networks p. 150)*.

continued on next page ›

KEY TACTIC

NUDITY

When the female elders fell naked to the ground, wailing and shouting, they made the ministers run away, ashamed. It reminded those male officials about how disgraceful they were being against those women, who were only trying to help sustain lives, like their own mothers did.

KEY PRINCIPLE

USE YOUR CULTURAL ASSETS

Stripping naked and pointing breasts at the enemy is a cultural omen in Acholi culture. It invokes the worst maledictions and great harm against those who do injustice. The curse of nakedness has proven very effective in helping movements strengthen the collective identity tied to the land.

RELATED

Boxing Gender Oppression » p. 20
Miniskirt March » p. 50

Civil disobedience » p. 108

Seek safety in support networks » p. 150

Postcolonialism » p. 196

Pillars of power » p. 210
Power mapping » p. 216
Spectrum of allies » p. 232

LEARN MORE

Meet the Ugandan Peasant Grandmother Who Terrifies Her President
| Phil Wilmot, Waging Nonviolence, 2015

Did Grandmothers Kill a Government Minister, Nonviolently?
| Phil Wilmot, Waging Nonviolence, 2016

Uganda: Amuru Women's Naked Power
| Joseph Were, The Independent, 2015

WELCOME TO PALESTINE

Ben-Gurion Airport/Lod Airport, Tel Aviv, Historic Palestine | 2011 - 2013

Hundreds of international solidarity activists staged a "fly-in" at Ben Gurion airport demanding to visit Palestine in protest of Israel's racist border policies and de facto siege of historic Palestine.

Ribal Al-Kurdi

The Palestinian people have been enduring systematic repression, colonization, and ethnic cleansing since the occupation of Palestine in 1948. Today, Palestinians live in Bantustan-like areas segregated by an apartheid wall built on stolen Palestinian land to allow Israeli settlers to enjoy Jewish-only privileges. Historic Palestine has been torn into scattered pieces of land disconnected from each other.

In 2011, Palestinians in the West Bank invited people of conscience from across the world to visit Palestine with the aim of drawing attention to the cruelty of life under the occupation, in general, and racist Israeli border policies, in particular. The initiative also aimed to strengthen the ongoing boycott effort to isolate Israel, demonstrate the hypocrisy and illegitimacy of the Israeli occupation and colonization of Palestine, and exert pressure on European and other governments accused of collaboration with that occupation.

Since Israeli authorities regularly deny visitors the right to visit Palestine if they state their intention to do so at the border, the idea was to have international solidarity activists fly into Tel Aviv's Ben Gurion airport, and try to publically exercise their right to visit Palestine. Inevitably, they would be denied that right,

International solidarity activists unfurling "Welcome to Palestine" banners upon arriving at Ben Gurion Airport/ Lod Airport. Photo: Activestills

"The actions disrupted the status quo at the heart of injustice, making a clear statement that could not be silenced except by repression."

which, if well-publicized, would help expose the truth about Israel's regime of occupation, colonization, and apartheid.

In the first year, more than 300 people from different countries and nationalities took part. After arriving at the airport, activists peacefully unfurled their "Welcome to Palestine" banners, creating a dramatic scene at the airport. Israeli police attacked the protesters, and ripped down their signs. Activists and non-activists alike were arrested and interrogated. Those identified as part of the campaign were deported or sent to detention facilities.

In response, the Israeli government launched a "diplomatic" campaign requesting governments of other countries to help bring an end to this form of solidarity. Some airlines cancelled the scheduled flights, others, at the behest of Israeli security, prevented activists from boarding planes for which they had already purchased tickets that they had every right to use.

In 2012, most of the 400 people worldwide who were set to fly to Palestine were denied boarding. Activists responded by holding sit-ins inside airports across Europe to protest their governments' complicity in supporting the Israeli occupation and violations of Palestinian human rights. During the sit-ins, activists also distributed flyers to raise awareness about the campaigns. In some of these airports, pro-Palestine protesters were violently dispersed and expelled from the airports.

All told, the actions disrupted the status quo at the heart of injustice, making a clear statement that could not be silenced except by repression. The extensive local and international media coverage exposed the repression and racism of Israeli policies, leading the Israeli regime to launch a massive PR campaign in an attempt to save face.

WHY IT WORKED

The Welcome to Palestine campaign came up with an innovative new tactic to expose the truth of Israel's racist border policies, and ushered in a unique type of solidarity. The organizers understood that it is much more effective to *show* an injustice, rather than just *tell* people about it. They also understood that quite often the key to success isn't what you do, but how your target *reacts* to what you do *(see: PRINCIPLE: The real action is your target's reaction)*. By simply and nonviolently stating their intention (and perfectly legitimate right) to visit Palestine, and knowing that the Israeli authorities would not only refuse it, but respond with repression and violence (and that the media would keenly cover such a scene), the campaign set up a perfect scenario to expose the truth about the Israeli regime *(see: PRINCIPLE: Make the invisible visible)*.

continued on next page ›

KEY TACTIC

SUBVERSIVE TRAVEL

Freedom of movement is a basic right denied to Palestinians. By deliberately trying to exercise that right, which required defying Israeli travel restrictions, the Welcome to Palestine campaign put a global spotlight on the racist border policies imposed by the Israeli occupation.

KEY PRINCIPLES

THE REAL ACTION IS YOUR TARGET'S REACTION

Welcome to Palestine activists knew they would be denied entry to Palestine once they'd explicitly stated their intentions. They knew how the Israeli regime would react, and so they planned their action accordingly. And that reaction did a better job of demonstrating the racist, oppressive, and colonial policies of the apartheid state than any critique could.

PLAY TO THE AUDIENCE THAT ISN'T THERE

When designing your action, keep in mind the people who aren't physically in the immediate vicinity of where the action is taking place. The fly-in action was planned to have global media reach; organizers were keenly aware that their primary audience was not witnessing it directly in the airport, but receiving it indirectly all across the world through TV and other media.

O O O O

KEY THEORY

DECOLONIZATION

The fly-in staged by international solidarity activists was a media big bang that challenged and exposed Israeli apartheid as one of many facets of the Zionist colonization of the indigenous Palestinian population. It was yet another example of grassroots disobedience to the ongoing colonization of Palestine. By exposing the racist border policies, the violence against solidarity activists, and collusion of Western governments, the action disrupted, even if only momentarily, the balance of power between colonizer and the colonized.

LEARN MORE

Welcome to Palestine | Wikipedia

Welcome to Palestine — If You Can Get In | The Guardian, 2011

Israel Bans "Flytilla" Activists but Hundreds Left in Europe | Ahram Online, 2012

RELATED

⅄ II O ⌐
Stolen Gas Campaign » *p. 72*

⅄ ⅄ ⅄ ⅄
Civil disobedience » *p. 108*
Subversive travel » *p. 130*

O O O O
Al faza'a (a surge of solidarity) » *p. 172*
Postcolonialism » *p. 196*

⌐ ⌐ ⌐ ⌐
Spectrum of allies » *p. 232*

YELLOW PIGS IN PARLIAMENT

Kampala, Uganda | 2014

In 2014, to protest government corruption and high rates of youth unemployment, young activists painted two pigs yellow (the color of the ruling party), and let them run wild in Uganda's Parliament.

Norman Tumuhimbise

In June 2014, President Yoweri K. Museveni and the Ugandan Parliament presented their State of the Nation address and their national budget, without ever mentioning the scandalous unemployment rate of 84 percent among Ugandan youths — more than 10 million young people, around a third of the country's population.

This provoked a small group of young activists to sneak two yellow-painted pigs (yellow is the color of the ruling party, the National Resistance Movement [NRM]) into Uganda's Parliament to protest government corruption and high rates of youth unemployment. This nonviolent action was inspired by similar protests in Kenya one year earlier, but this time activists took more of a prankster approach, releasing the pigs inside, rather than outside, Parliament.

Pigs are known for their greedy and sometimes cannibalistic behavior — when they are hungry, they sometimes eat their own piglets. The message of the protest: Museveni's government acts similarly, "eating Uganda's young people" to feed their own greed. The two pigs represented the president and the prime minister, who were responsible for this catastrophic situation and were the main beneficiaries of corruption.

The Ugandan Parliament was chosen as the site of the demonstration because it's the place where all governmental institutions and decision makers meet to discuss and pass the laws that perpetuate corruption, injustice, oppression, and exploitation. The pigs had slogans pinned to their ears condemning corruption. And the two young activists who released them wore white T-shirts with red letters denouncing youth unemployment, corruption, and government extravagance.

By equating the dictatorial president and the prime minister with pigs, the action was designed to shame Uganda's two top rulers as corrupt, and denounce their

> *"Sometimes laughter can be the most effective way to dispel people's fear or complacency and puncture a leader's aura of invincibility."*

permanent neglect of the youth situation. Unexpectedly, however, the media and public attention that resulted focused much more on the security breach and the mockery it made of the government's boasts about its strong security policies. This turned out to not be all bad, as making such a fool of his security forces undressed the dictator completely and created an embarrassing enough situation that the country's inspector general of police had to come in and investigate. In the end, the action sparked widespread attention and debate, and the people behind the action were constantly invited to radio and TV programs to talk about the yellow pigs protest, which brought many opportunities to spread their intended message, possibly to an even broader audience than they would otherwise have had.

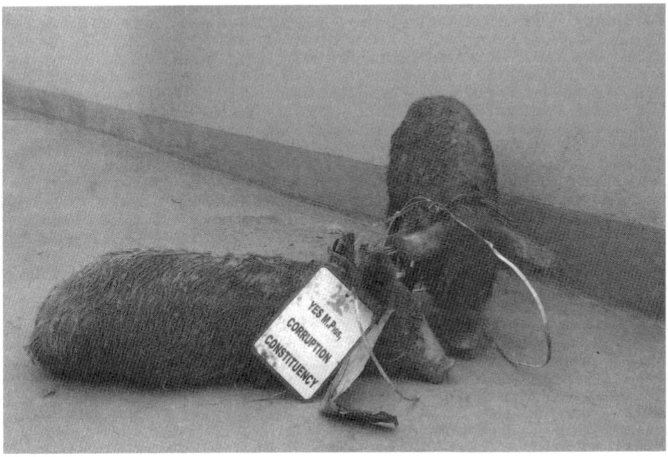

These pigs made quite an impression during their political debut, creatively disrupting parliamentary proceedings while squealing truth to power. Photo: Agence France-Presse/Getty Images

⅄ ⅄ ⅄ ⅄

KEY TACTIC

CREATIVE DISRUPTION

By bringing an unruly beast into the halls of power, the yellow pigs protest shattered decorum, undermined authority, and caused a national scandal. But it was more than disruption for disruption's sake; it was symbolically effective disruption informed by a sharp understanding of Uganda's culture and ethics. There was no better symbol of corruption run amok at the highest levels of power than a greedy, cannibalistic pig painted in the ruling party's colors scampering through the Parliament.

II II II II

KEY PRINCIPLE

USE HUMOR TO UNDERMINE AUTHORITY

President Museveni has consistently tried to portray himself as invincible, going so far to call himself *Sebalwanyi* (loosely meaning "warrior of warriors"). By showing how easily pigs could enter and wander the halls of the parliament building without being noticed, the action undercut this overblown image and widely exposed him to ridicule. Sometimes laughter can be the most effective way to dispel people's fear or complacency and puncture the leader's aura of invincibility.

RELATED

⅄ II O ⌐

Honk at Parliament » p. 44

II II II II

Use humor to undermine authority » p. 160

WHY IT WORKED

The demonstration succeeded because of months of meticulous planning. The young activists created a cover story that one of them was carrying out research for a friend working at Parliament that required them to meet regularly. His regular visits allowed him to become friendly with the security guards. By successfully pulling off the highly visual action, the activists captured the public imagination, using humor and daring to shame corrupt politicians.

WHY IT FAILED

In spite of the excellent use of symbolism (pigs = corruption; yellow = ruling party), media and public attention focused more on the breach of security that permitted the youths to smuggle pigs into Parliament, and less on the corruption and unemployment the action was meant to highlight. Though the action succeeded in attracting widespread public attention, it was less successful at achieving its intended result: to put corruption and unemployment at the center of the media coverage of the national budget.

LEARN MORE

Firsthand Account of the Yellow Pig Demonstration
| Norman Tumuhimbise, Unsowing the Mustard Seed, 2015

In Uganda, an Activist's Resurrection Is a Victory for a Growing Movement
| Phil Wilmot, Waging Nonviolence, 2015

ZAPATISTA CARAVAN

Chiapas and Mexico City, Mexico | 1994-1996

In 1994, university students organized educational brigades to break the information blockade and rumors about the uprising of the Zapatista Army for National Liberation (EZLN).

"For everyone, the light. For everyone everything. For us pain and anguish, for us the joy of rebellion, for us a future denied, for us the dignity of insurrection. For us nothing."
—Subcomandante Insurgente Marcos

Abraham García Gárate and Sergio Beltrán

On January 1, 1994, in the southeast of Mexico, the uprising of the Zapatista Army for National Liberation (EZLN) began on the same day that the North American Free Trade Agreement (NAFTA) took effect. The revolt of the EZLN made evident that the recent neoliberal reforms enacted by the PRI, Mexico's corrupt ruling party, had left a large gap among social sectors of society, with indigenous peoples and peasants being the most marginalized.

One of the firsts groups to stand in solidarity with the demands of the Zapatistas were students. In the various schools and campuses of the Autonomous National University of Mexico (UNAM), students quickly began holding meetings and leading educational brigades to inform their peers about the uprising in Chiapas. Thus, organized students amplified the voice of the indigenous movement in order to break the blockade of disinformation and rumors that commercial mass media, together with the government, erected between the people and the EZLN.

"University students found in Zapatistas what nobody in the Mexican political class could offer: honesty."

In this context was born, on June 19, 1994, the Ricardo Pozas University Caravan (named after the Mexican anthropologist Ricardo Pozas Horcasitas, whose writings had provided a clear description of the conditions of the indigenous Tzotziles in the highlands of Chiapas), also known as the Zapatista Caravan. Led by members of the University Student Council, several student organizations took on the task of organizing the First Rock Festival for Peace and Tolerance, a massive music concert inside the university campus that promoted the gathering of two autonomous movements of the country: the university community and the indigenous peoples of Mexico, whose aspirations were reflected in the Zapatista demands.

In the presence of massive numbers of young people from all social sectors, an agreement was reached for the student movement to support and spread information about the EZLN movement. The bond of solidarity and trust between the young people from the Caravan and the Zapatistas became so strong that some were invited to act as consultants for the EZLN in peace talks with the government.

University students found in the Zapatistas what nobody else in the Mexican political class could offer — honesty. From that first concert in 1994 until the Zapatistas' national consultation of 1997, the Caravan accompanied all activities organized by EZLN, embracing Zapatista slogans and ideas, specifically *leading by obeying* and *everything for everyone, and nothing for ourselves.*

The youth movement in general, and specifically the student movement, learned from their solidarity with the indigenous uprising that their demands and struggles should not just focus on issues of public education, but also on the national demands they shared with all marginalized sectors. For its part, the EZLN gained a bridge that allowed them to share their message more widely, in diverse and creative ways, making it strongly visible in different sectors of Mexican society and around the world *(see: PRINCIPLE: Seek safety in support networks p. 150).*

WHY IT WORKED

The Ricardo Pozas University Caravan managed to bring together diverse organizations and student groups inside and outside the UNAM with a common goal: to share the story and practices of the Zapatista uprising, and to organize a broad and diverse solidarity network with the Zapatista communities. It also worked because it made space for different movements and individual student struggles, especially in public universities located mainly in Mexico City (UNAM, UAM, Politécnico).

WHY IT FAILED

Many of the participants eventually drifted from the Zapatista ideals as they moved into careers. Some were integrated into public life, participating directly in political parties (mainly the moderate leftist PRD), and would tout their involvement in the Caravan as part of their resumé as professional politicians.

Zapatista family. Photo: Eduardo Velasco Vazquez | @lalo777

⅄ ⅄ ⅄ ⅄

KEY TACTIC

VISIBILITY ACTION

One of the most useful tactics employed was the alliance with political musicians who also supported the Zapatistas. Together they managed to reach an audience far more vast than either group would have reached separately.

| | | | | | | |

KEY PRINCIPLES

EVERYTHING FOR EVERYONE, AND NOTHING FOR OURSELVES

Perhaps the principle that best illustrates the life and spirit of the Ricardo Pozas University Caravan was one taught by the Zapatistas themselves. The struggle for autonomy is a political struggle in the service of all, and not only for the participants of the movement.

RELATED

Burmese Students' Long March » *p. 26*
Schools of Struggle » *p. 60*

Seek safety in support networks » *p. 150*

Neoliberalism » *p. 192*
The Global South » *p. 188*

Spectrum of allies » *p. 232*

KEY THEORY

INTERSECTIONALITY

The solidarity of students with the historically marginalized and discriminated indigenous movement served to strengthen both movements and helped participants to find a role for themselves in a common and wider struggle for autonomy and against inequality and injustice.

LEARN MORE

We Make the Road by Walking: Lessons from the Zapatista Caravan
| Rachel Neumann, Monthly Review, 2001

TACTICS

Specific forms of creative action, such as a flash mob or a blockade.

"Tactics . . . lack a specific location, survive through improvisation, and use the advantages of the weak against the strong."

—Paul Lewis

Every discipline has its forms of action: ballet dancers lunge and pirouette; boxers throw jabs and uppercuts. Likewise, creative activists have their own forms of action. Some, like a sit-in, march, or picket line, have been used for generations. Others, like flash mobs and hashtag campaigns, are recent innovations. As with ballet or boxing, a single tactic, no matter how well executed, rarely wins the day. Victory comes, if it comes, through their artful combination.

CIVIL DISOBEDIENCE

Civil disobedience is the public and ethically motivated breaking of a law in order to challenge either the legitimacy of the specific law you're breaking or a greater injustice committed by the state.

"Civil disobedience is not our problem. Our problem is civil obedience."
—Howard Zinn

Søren Warburg

The greatest strength of social movements is often their capacity to disrupt. At its core, an act of civil disobedience is a disruption that expresses political opposition beyond what the law permits. In an act of civil disobedience, you either publicly break an unjust law in order to challenge the legitimacy of that law, or you commit some minor infraction (trespassing, for example, or obstruction), with the intent of bringing about broader political changes.

Civil disobedience can manifest in a number of different ways. Strikes, sit-ins or sit-downs, marches, and lockdowns, among many other tactics, can all be used as acts of civil disobedience.

Because it seeks to awaken the conscience of society to some injustice, an act of civil disobedience should be carefully planned if it is to have maximum effect. Design your action so that it places your target in a decision dilemma or uses humor to undermine their authority. Be public about your intent, maintain nonviolent discipline, and be prepared to go to jail *(see: TACTIC: Jail solidarity p. 118)*.

Though nonviolent resistance to injustice is as old as injustice itself (as the classic Greek tragedy *Antigone* tells us), the modern understanding of civil disobedience dates to Henry David Thoreau's book *Civil Disobedience* (1849). Thoreau argued that the individual has a right to resist government abuses and injustices, stating, "the only obligation which I have a right to assume is to do at any time what I think right." He refused to pay his taxes because they were being used to expand slavery in the United States and wage a war against Mexico. A century later, Hannah Arendt argued that civil disobedience is integral to a democratic state, since only "extralegal action," such as civil disobedience, can expand rights and justice beyond the existing limits of the law.

Acts of civil disobedience can challenge not just a specific law, but also the very legitimacy of a state — particularly a colonial or occupying power *(see: THEORY: Decolonization)*. Indeed, one of the best known examples of civil disobedience is Gandhi's salt march from Ahmedabad to Dandi to make salt in violation of the wildly unpopular British salt laws, a campaign that played a key role in exposing the illegitimacy of British authority and ultimately led to India's independence *(see: STORY: The Salt March)*. This act of civil disobedience was brilliantly planned and strategically well thought-out. Gandhi crisscrossed the country for weeks, publicly announcing the impending "crime" and telling his fellow Indians that it was their duty to disobey British rule by marching with him. This put the British authorities in a decision dilemma: If they arrested the salty lawbreakers, it would spark even wider support for the movement and confirm the British rulers' brutality *(see: PRINCIPLE: Put your target in a decision dilemma)*. But if they didn't do anything, they would look as if they had lost the ability to enforce their own laws. Either way, British rule was doomed by Gandhi's mass public violation of a simple law.

This photo by Soe Zeya Tun/Reuters captures the power and joy of civil disobedience in service of a moral cause, as student protesters cheer before trying to break a police line in Letpadan, Myanmar.

KEY PRINCIPLE

MAINTAIN NONVIOLENT DISCIPLINE

If participants in an act of civil disobedience become violent, you have already lost. The power of civil disobedience lies in a respect for a moral law that is more powerful than the state's laws, and you need to hold the moral high ground *(see: PRINCIPLE: Anger works best when you have the moral high ground)*. To be effective, you must ensure that everyone participating is committed to nonviolence during the action *(see: THEORY: Strategic nonviolence)*. Otherwise, you will only bolster the legitimacy of the state, and give them an excuse to beat up the "common lawbreaker." If you stay cool and disciplined, you will have a much higher chance of winning the respect and support of the public than if you don't *(see: THEORY: Hamoq and hamas)*.

POTENTIAL RISKS

An act of civil disobedience is by definition a breaking of a law, so the risk of being arrested is pretty high. You should expect arrest, and plan accordingly. Make sure your group is prepared to offer jail solidarity. If the state is particularly brutal or if you are a member of an oppressed group, the stakes of breaking the law are naturally higher and the ability to awaken the conscience of the broader public is often more limited. Build a support network that will be able to apply pressure on the authorities in order to deter harsh sentences or violence against you *(see: PRINCIPLE: Seek safety in support networks p. 150)*. Research whether there are international mechanisms that you can use to apply pressure on your behalf *(see: PRINCIPLE: Activate international mechanisms p. 138)*.

RELATED

Burmese Students' Long March » p. 26
Schools of Struggle » p. 60
Sign Language Sit-In » p. 66
Stop Prawer Plan » p. 78
Welcome to Palestine » p. 90

Jail solidarity » p. 118
Subversive travel » p. 130

Activate international mechanisms » p. 138
Seek safety in support networks » p. 150
Use humor to undermine authority » p. 160
Would you like some structure with your momentum? » p. 166

Postcolonialism » p. 196

Pillars of power » p. 210
SMART objectives » p. 226

LEARN MORE

Civil Disobedience Resources | ActUp

Letter from Birmingham Jail | Martin Luther King, 1963

人 人 人 人

DIVESTMENT

A divestment campaign is an effective way to apply economic pressure on an industry or state that is profiting from injustice and destruction.

"The logic of divestment couldn't be simpler: If it's wrong to wreck the climate, it's wrong to profit from that wreckage."
—Bill McKibben

"Those who invest in South Africa should not think they are doing us a favor; they are here for what they get out of our cheap and abundant labor, and they should know that they are buttressing one of the most vicious systems."
—Archbishop Desmond Tutu

⚠

Hoda Baraka and Mahmoud Nawajaa

A divestment campaign is an effective way to apply economic pressure on an industry or state that is profiting from injustice and destruction. The idea is that stock sell-offs, cancelled contracts, and the like will scare off potential investors and create enough economic pressure to compel the target to comply with your demands. A divestment campaign helps to politically isolate the target and limit its ability to act with impunity.

The tactic became prominent in the 1980s, when it was used to bring concentrated economic pressure on the government of South Africa, helping to force it to abolish its racist policy and crime of apartheid. The tactic has most recently been taken up by Palestine solidarity activists and by the global climate justice movement. Both campaigns have shed light on the power and versatility of a divestment strategy.

The global climate justice movement has chosen to target the fossil fuel industry, identifying it as the main obstacle blocking serious action on climate change. The 2015 climate talks in Paris saw 500 institutions commit to divest their capital from fossil fuel companies, while many students have launched campaigns pressuring the universities they attend to divest. So far, the movement has won pledges to divest $3.4 trillion — a sign that the tide of public opinion is turning against the fossil fuel industry.

Often, a divestment campaign will focus on *secondary targets* because the *primary target* is too powerful or too removed from your supporters' daily lives to be directly pressured *(see: STORY: Taco Bell Boycott)*. This is how the Palestinian-led Boycott, Divestment, and Sanctions (BDS) movement has operated. In 2008, for instance, the BDS movement called for divestment from Veolia, a French multinational company that was involved in building a light rail system in Palestine that would connect Jerusalem with illegal settlements, thereby contravening international law and Palestinian human rights. After mounting pressure from

This 1987 image of students calling on Pennsylvania State University to divest from companies doing business in South Africa dramatized one of the first successful uses of the tactic. Photo: Craig Houtz, Associated Press

people of conscience across the world and having lost billions of dollars worth of global contracts, in 2015 Veolia officially declared that it would end all its business in Israel's occupation of Palestine *(see: STORY: Dump Veolia Campaign)*. Through many similar victories against businesses that profit from Israel's regime of colonialism, occupation, and apartheid, the BDS movement is mounting significant pressure on Israel to comply with international law — far more than it could have brought to bear by focusing only on its primary target.

Potentially, any company or institution can become a target of a divestment campaign, but it is absolutely critical that the target is chosen strategically *(see: PRINCIPLE: Choose your target wisely)*. Once a target is chosen, power map the web of relationships around that target *(see: METHODOLOGY: Power mapping p. 216)*. In weighing the range of primary and secondary targets, organizers should consider the degree of involvement of each potential target in the violations at hand, and how vulnerable the target might be to pressure or persuasion.

While the core focus of a divestment campaigns is to bring direct or indirect economic pressure on a target, the campaign's most important function is often more broadly political and moral. The South African divestment campaign helped to politically isolate the apartheid regime. The BDS movement is successfully forcing wider and wider sectors of global public opinion to confront the criminality of Israel's occupation and colonization of historic Palestine. From museums, to college campuses, to investment firms, the global fossil fuel divestment movement is successfully turning the fossil fuel sector into a rogue industry and revoking its social license. Furthermore, because these divestment campaigns simultaneously draw a clear ethical line in the sand and offer many local targets, and therefore create many points of entry *(see: PRINCIPLE: Create many points of entry)*, they have been particularly effective at deepening and broadening the movements they're part of.

Almost all entities being lobbied to divest will initially resist or ignore your call. It is thus important to remain persistent and have an escalation plan you can stick to until your target concedes to your demands *(see: PRINCIPLE: Escalate strategically)*. Remember: A divestment campaign is only one piece of a long-term, multi-pronged strategy, and the breakthrough will come only after a trickle of small successes that continue to accumulate until the last straw breaks the camel's back — and you win.

POTENTIAL RISKS

Targets will often try to deflate your enthusiasm, momentum, or anger by making misleading statements and false promises. Divestment is a long-term campaign that requires patience and persistence. The pressure must continue until the actual goal is achieved.

KEY PRINCIPLE

PERSONALIZE AND POLARIZE

Divestment focuses on one secondary target at a time (e.g. the Tate Museum's sponsorship of British Petroleum) in order to increase pressure and build public anger against the primary target (e.g. the fossil fuel industry as a whole), so that it becomes isolated and eventually has no choice but to comply. People start to personally identify the primary target with the injustice you are fighting, eventually seeing it as the main obstacle to a just solution. The idea is to dismantle the network of support that your target enjoys, including clients, sponsors, shareholders, or the general public, until the target accedes to your campaign's demands.

RELATED

The Global South » p. 188

Pillars of power » p. 210
Power mapping » p. 216
Spectrum of allies » p. 232

LEARN MORE

Interview: The Man Behind the BDS Movement | Rami Younis, +972 Magazine, 2015

The Case for Fossil Fuel Divestment | Bill McKibben, Rolling Stone, 2013

What is Fossil Fuel Divestment? | Go Fossil Free

Private Prison Divestment Campaign Resources | ENLACE: Organizing for racial and economic justice

BDS Divestment Page | BDS movement

JAIL SOLIDARITY

Jail solidarity involves putting pressure on authorities after activists are arrested. It seeks to create a strong community of resistance in order to stop the persecution of activists and deter state violence.

"If you want to know who your friends are, get yourself a jail sentence."
—Charles Bukowski

"I have the people behind me and the people are my strength."
—Huey Newton

McDonald Lewanika

Political imprisonment has long been a standard repressive response from state authorities, particularly tyrannical regimes and authoritarian governments, to criminalize dissent, spread fear, break rebellions, and stop the growth of social movements.

Jail solidarity is a tactic for putting pressure on authorities after activists are arrested. By pushing for activists' release, or, failing that, for decent treatment and protection from psychological and physical abuse, it seeks to create a strong community of resistance, based on mutual support and unity of purpose, that can act against harassment, false accusations, selective prosecutions, strategies of isolation and victimization, and other forms of persecution.

The tactic can be applied in two interconnected ways: one, within the prison walls among arrested activists, and two, spanning those walls to connect prisoners with those on the outside who support them. The aim in the first case is to agitate for fair and equal treatment for all activists arrested, protect those who cannot afford to pay their way out of jail, and prevent abuses of the justice system, particularly those targeting the poor, youth, and minorities. Withholding names and other forms of identification, and collectively refusing any plea unless it helps to negotiate the dismissal or reduction of charges for everyone, are key components for this tactic to be effective.

Activists in Melbourne, Australia, gathered to call for the release of Pussy Riot, a Russian feminist punk-rock collective who had been jailed in Russia and were facing charges of "hooliganism," which carries a seven-year prison term. Photo: Mark Burban | CC BY-NC 2.0

In the second case, there are many ways people outside the jail can support prisoners, but visiting with care packages is often the most crucial. Care packages supply food and water for arrested activists, but also create a moment of interaction that often helps to facilitate legal, medical, psychological, social, and spiritual support. These visits have the additional purpose of ensuring the activists are being treated with dignity and are not being abused or tortured. It shows both the jailed and the jailers that there are people on the outside looking out for them, and that they will raise the alarm if they detect any abusive practices.

This public support is important because, if it's organized, it can put massive pressure on the state to release the prisoners. During visiting hours, people can organize to show up all at the same time. By flooding the jail with visitors, organizers show the authorities that arresting activists will not stop them fighting for their causes. While revolutionaries can be arrested, the revolution can never be.

Jail solidarity breaks the fear barrier created by isolation, creates a community of support, and amplifies the message behind the original arrest, helping to raise issues that were invisible prior to the activist's imprisonment. It undermines the state's effort to silence dissent and transforms an otherwise unbearable incarceration into something bearable, even powerful.

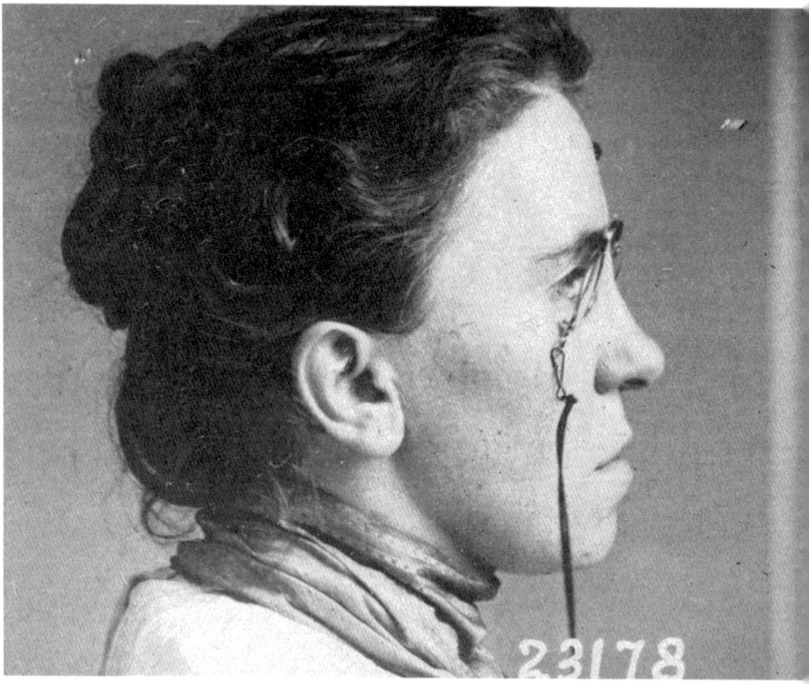

POTENTIAL RISKS

To work, jail solidarity requires, well, solidarity. Differences of strategy can pull a group of arrestees apart; for instance, when some people want to keep resisting inside the jails while others think it's most important to get out and make a stand on the streets. Within a group of arrestees, different individual circumstances, especially different levels of privilege and risk tolerance, can work against solidarity. Some arrestees cannot handle the precarious and unhealthy conditions in the jails; others cannot afford the time jail solidarity demands, as it often takes a long time to force the authorities' hands.

Without jail solidarity among those arrested, however, the power to make decisions is transferred to the judicial system in a way that is risky for activists — both individually, and for future collective engagements. When an arrested activist decides to break jail solidarity and make a deal to get released, the key question is: How will this decision impact those who stay behind? Once outside, that individual can continue to support those inside by speaking to the media and carrying messages to families and other supporters, but that requires a conscious and often long-term commitment. A final risk: In some countries, jails are legally defined as protected areas, so any protests organized on the inside are considered illegal and can lead to further arrests.

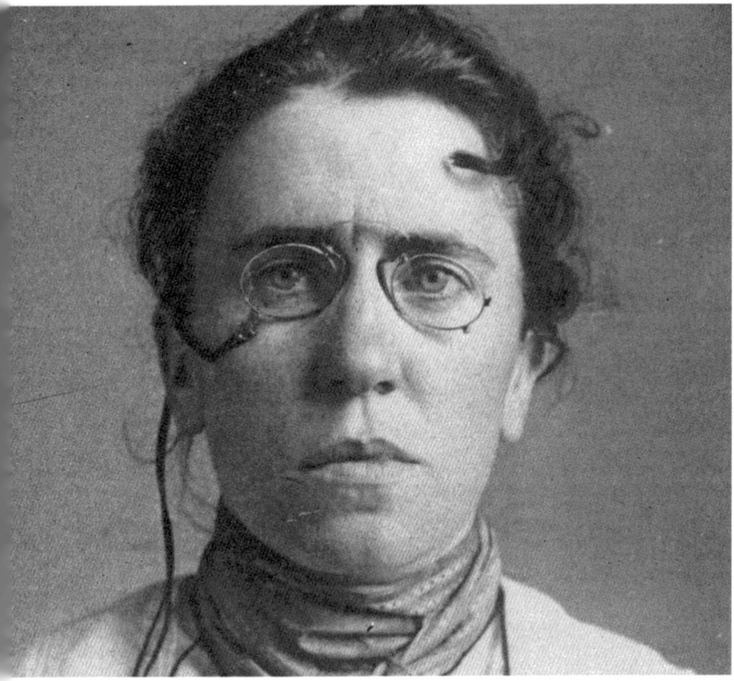

"When a law has outgrown time and necessity, it must go," renowned anarchist Emma Goldman declared a few days after her arrest for distributing information about birth control. "And the only way to get rid of the law is to awaken the public to the fact that it has outlived its purpose, and that is precisely what I have been doing and mean to do in the future."

KEY PRINCIPLE

SEEK SAFETY IN PUBLICITY

Abuse of power thrives in the shadows. Sometimes the best way to ensure that the arrested or disappeared person is returned safely is simply to make as much noise as possible as early as possible, identifying the responsible party and ensuring that they will be held accountable for any abuses. Media coverage, phone banking campaigns targeting the responsible authorities, and international action appeals can all help to ensure the safety of those arrested, and help deter further violence.

RELATED

Civil disobedience » *p. 108*

Activate international mechanisms » *p. 138*
Seek safety in support networks » *p. 150*

Pillars of power » *p. 210*

LEARN MORE

The Global Justice Movement's Use of "Jail Solidarity" as a Response to Police Repression and Arrest: An Ethnographic Study | Beverly Yuen Thompson, Qualitative Inquiry, 2007

Jail Support and Solidarity | Midnight Special and Katya Komisaruk, Organizing for Power

Jail Solidarity | Civil Disobedience Training, ACT UP

MUSIC VIDEO

Social justice music videos combine the contagious power of music with compelling visuals to expose injustice and inspire potential allies into action.

Emily Hong

Music has long played an important role in generating and sustaining activist communities and social movements. Social justice music videos take this power a step further, combining the contagious power of music with compelling visuals to expose injustice and inspire potential allies into action. Typically a result of collaboration among musicians, activists, and videographers, social justice music videos transform a classic tool — protest music — for 21st-century community organizing and mass mobilization in the Global South.

In high-risk political contexts, social justice music videos can literally break the silence and prepare the ground for local organizing. In northern Myanmar (also known as Burma), rock band BLAST teamed up with All Kachin Students and Youth Union, Kachin Development Networking Group, and Kachin News Group to release a 2010 karaoke music video album highlighting an emergent environmental crisis. Two hit songs, "Aka Law" and "Malikha," gave voice to the cries of the Mali river,

Sofia Ashraf rapping in Kodaikanal Won't. Photo: screenshot from YouTube video

bringing attention to the ecological and cultural havoc wreaked by the Chinese-built Myitsone Dam. Local and national coalitions were able to build on the widespread awareness of the dam's destructive impacts to mount a successful campaign that saw the dam's construction suspended in 2011.

In certain instances, a viral music video can turn a small campaign into a transnational sensation — bringing in key new allies that can shift the balance of power. In 2015, South Indian rapper Sofia Ashraf and Vettiver Collective repurposed Nicki Minaj's "Anaconda," calling out Unilever for its mercury contamination in Kodaikanal, Tamil Nadu. The resulting video, "Kodaikanal Won't," went viral, gaining close to 4 million views and a surge in signatures for an online petition demanding justice for poisoned former employees. The video catapulted 15 years of local organizing efforts onto an international stage, giving the struggle new transnational allies and media coverage. Months of intensified campaigning and a boycott of Unilever products forced the company to do the previously unthinkable: compensate Kodaikanal workers.

Social justice music videos have not only remixed popular songs or genres from the Global North, but have also contributed to the revival of indigenous and traditional languages, music, dance, and storytelling. A stunning video from New York-based art collective Semillas (Seeds), for example, channeled the power of indigenous danza, hip hop, and ballet to tell the story of the 43 disappeared Ayotzinapa students from Mexico.

While high-budget productions with high-profile musicians can certainly command an audience (see MIA's 2015 "Borders" video on the refugee crisis), low-budget videos can be just as powerful. "Kodaikanal Won't" was shot in just one day. In areas with limited or slow internet access, low-resolution karaoke video compact discs (VCDs) can be cheaply reproduced, circulated through underground networks, or sold on street corners.

Music videos can take on a range of issues more effectively than speech alone. Audio-visuals can subvert dominant narratives by contesting government claims with visible, on-the-ground impacts. Such sensory details can work in tandem with powerful lyrics that call out the hypocrisy of power-holders, such as corporations sensitive to consumer power or governments shamed by citizen voices. While activist indignation doesn't often find productive channels, musical genres such as rock and hip-hop provide rhythmic openings to channel anger in ways that can move hard-to-reach allies and power-holders *(see: THEORY: Hamoq and hamas).*

continued on next page ›

English-Sri Lankan Tamil rapper M.I.A.'s lyrics and videos tackle a range of social and political issues. Photo: Moses | CC BY 2.0

KEY PRINCIPLE

SHIFT THE SPECTRUM OF ALLIES

A well-planned music video can serve as an impactful organizing tool to activate much-needed allies. For example, "Kodaikanal Won't" succeeded in mobilizing transnational solidarity for a long-term local campaign. In doing so, the video shifted passive international allies into active ones, mobilizing thousands to take social media actions and boycott Unilever products. The result was a global PR mess that left Unilever no choice but to finally settle with its poisoned former employees.

RELATED

Stolen Gas Campaign » *p. 72*

Use humor to undermine authority » *p. 160*

Postcolonialism » *p. 196*

Spectrum of allies » *p. 232*

LEARN MORE

Never Thought "Kodaikanal Won't" Video Could Make Unilever Settle: Rapper Sofia Ashraf | Tushar Kaushik, The New Indian Express

M.I.A. Talks About the "Borders" Video and Why She's Getting Legal Threats for a Soccer Jersey | Ryan Bassil, Noisey, 2016

The Justice Through Music Project

SUBVERSIVE TRAVEL

Subversive travel seeks to defy and subvert unjust travel restrictions. It can be used to facilitate freedom of movement, challenge militarized borders, break a siege, deliver aid, or attract media attention.

"I was the conductor of the Underground Railroad for eight years, and I can say what most conductors can't say — I never ran my train off the track and I never lost a passenger."
—*Harriet Tubman*

D. 'Alwan

Subversive travel seeks to defy, subvert, and expose unjust travel restrictions. It can be used to facilitate freedom of movement, challenge militarized borders, break a siege, or deliver aid. Subversive travel may provoke a response by authorities and can garner mainstream media attention, as in the case of travel ban challenges, or lend safety to communities at risk, as in the case of "human shield" delegations.

Important subversive travel antecedents include the Underground Railroad, a network of covert routes and safe houses used by 19th-century enslaved people of African descent in the United States escaping to free states and Canada, and the Kindertransport (Children's Transport), a series of rescue efforts that brought thousands of refugee Jewish children to Great Britain from Nazi Germany between 1938 and 1940.

From El Salvador to Sri Lanka, when facing extreme violence and state repression that seems insurmountable, movement organizers have invited Western activists to join them in solidarity, offering some protection as international observers or human shields, and helping to shine a global news spotlight on the issues *(see: PRINCIPLE: Seek safety in support networks p. 150)*. US-based organizations such as Global Exchange and CODEPINK have coordinated civilian delegations to Cuba, in violation of the US embargo, as a means of protesting the economic strangulation of that country. Women On Waves (WOW), a Netherlands-registered ship, sails to countries where abortions are illegal, in order that WOW medical staff can safely provide early-term abortions aboard the ship, while in international waters.

The Israeli government's strict travel restrictions have made it a frequent target of subversive travel actions. The Free Gaza Movement launched flotillas carrying only humanitarian aid and human rights workers that attempted to break the naval blockade imposed by Israel on the Gaza Strip. Birthright Unplugged turned the tables on "Birthright Israel" trips by inviting all people, not just Jews, to travel to Israel and Palestine, while Birthright RePlugged facilitated trips for Palestinian children living in refugee camps to travel through checkpoints without documentation to see Jerusalem and their ancestors' lands *(see: STORY: Birthright Unplugged/Replugged)*. In the cases of the Free Gaza Movement and Birthright RePlugged, this travel is legal under international law but denied by Israel. In such cases, the journey becomes the destination.

Palestinian children living in refugee camps study a pre-1948 map of Palestinian villages to find their ancestral village that was destroyed by Israel. Photo: D. 'Alwan

Welcome to Palestine is yet another example. In 2011, Palestinian civil society invited internationals to visit Palestine. When asked by Israeli border security, travelers were encouraged to say they were going to Palestine (knowing they would be refused entry). As a result, 130 activists were denied entry, deported, jailed, or coerced into signing documents pledging not to participate in political actions. This action made headlines and helped educate people on Israeli injustices *(see: STORY: Welcome to Palestine p. 90).*

Finally, the UndocuBus tour brought people living in the United States without documentation together to openly tour the country, declaring, "No one is illegal." By outing themselves as undocumented people, these activists courageously exposed themselves to potential arrest or deportation in the name of calling attention to the urgent need for immigration reform.

Diverse acts of subversive travel are ubiquitous in activist practice, both past and present. Not only is it a way to challenge the authorities when they deny the fundamental human right to freedom of movement, but it can also engage the revolutionary imagination to envision what a future state of freedom might look like.

POTENTIAL RISKS

Risks may include detention, denial of entry, deportation, abuse, and harm. Also, without a clear anti-oppression analysis, the story that emerges from a subversive travel act may focus on the actions of, and potential repercussions on, the Western participants, rather than exposing ongoing repression and lack of freedom of movement for the most impacted population *(see: THEORY: Anti-oppression)*. For example, an activist gets arrested at the Israeli airport in Tel Aviv and, when interviewed by the media, instead of using the spotlight to direct an interview to a Palestinian activist, dramatizes their own experience without acknowledging that indigenous Palestinian people can't enter their own country *(see: PRINCIPLE: Take leadership from the most impacted)*.

continued on next page ›

I I I I I I I I

KEY PRINCIPLES

MAKE THE INVISIBLE VISIBLE

Travel restrictions are not always apparent to those not being restricted. By publicizing politicized barriers, subversive travel can make these types of unjust restrictions visible to a broader public. Increased visibility is often necessary for increased traction on an issue.

IF PROTEST IS MADE ILLEGAL, MAKE DAILY LIFE A PROTEST

When freedom of movement is restricted and the basic human right to travel is made illegal, just exercizing your right to travel, or even simply announcing your intention to defy a travel restriction, becomes an act of protest. In this way, travel becomes a subversive act.

RELATED

Welcome to Palestine » p. 90

Civil disobedience » p. 108

Seek safety in support networks » p. 150

Postcolonialism » p. 196

Spectrum of allies » p. 232

The Free Gaza Movement launched humanitarian flotillas that attempted to break the naval blockade imposed by Israel on the Gaza Strip. Here, the first flotilla is welcomed by Palestinians from Gaza. Photo: Sharyn Lock

LEARN MORE

The UndocuBus

Women on Waves

PRINCIPLES

Time-tested guidelines for designing successful actions and campaigns.

"Knowledge emerges only through invention and reinvention, through the restless, impatient, continuing, hopeful inquiry human beings pursue in the world, with the world, and with each other."

—Paulo Freire

After decades of battles won and lost, veteran creative activists tend to acquire a set of mental shortcuts for how to design successful actions and campaigns. These hard-won insights are not strict rules, but rather loose guidelines to keep in mind as you design your own actions.

ACTIVATE INTERNATIONAL MECHANISMS

While international mechanisms like the United Nations' human rights protocols are no cure-all, savvy campaigners can use them to help protect activists and to legitimate local struggles.

Ben Leather

Is your government violating human rights and ignoring your calls to stop abuses? Might international pressure be just the thing to persuade them to change? Are you keen to grab the world's attention, but unsure how? Activating international United Nations (UN) mechanisms might be the way to go.

The UN's array of organizations and acronyms can seem far removed from our day-to-day struggles for justice, but there are a number of international mechanisms that exist to support you in pressuring your government and other key actors to protect your rights and defend your work. The trick is to understand what these mechanisms can and can't do, and how you can activate them. Remember: These mechanisms are not a cure-all, just another tool in your toolbox.

First, seek guidance.
Find out which non-governmental organizations (NGOs) in your country are already interacting with the UN, and ask for their support. The UN's human rights office has a civil society section, with resources and staff to answer your questions, while independent organizations like the International Service for Human Rights (ISHR) publish handbooks, produce regular updates, and provide training on how to use the UN to strategically support grassroots struggles. You can also find out online what the UN has said previously about your country or the issue you work on.

Second, analyze how susceptible your government is to UN pressure.
Would the voice of international authorities give your local movement the additional weight it needs to be heard in the media? Would local politicians feel compelled to respond to forthright criticism from their peers in the UN sphere? Are local courts likely to reference international guidance and precedents in their decisions? Playing the UN game requires varying amounts of time and trouble, so you should make sure that its outcomes will be worth the effort.

Third, identify which mechanisms to activate and how to do so.
A UN expert (or "Special Procedures" as they are officially known) might well speak out about a human rights abuse if short, accurate, and well-documented information is sent in a timely manner. In Australia, for example, local NGOs used a press release by a group of UN experts to tip the scales in their struggle against repressive protest laws favoring big business over grassroots movements.

A panorama of the United Nations General Assembly. Photo: Spiff | CC BY-SA

Alternatively, you might persuade other countries to make recommendations related to your cause when your country comes up for its five-year UN Universal Periodic Review. In 2009, various countries used the Universal Periodic Review to criticize Mexico's lack of protection for threatened activists. Its government subsequently created a protection program. When this wasn't properly implemented, civil society ensured that 40 percent of member states spoke out about it, pressuring Mexico at their subsequent review.

If your country has ratified key treaties, it will be regularly assessed as to how well it is implementing its obligations, in regards to, say, women's equality or children's rights. In fact, if it has agreed to optional protocols, you might even be able to take a case of an individual violation to one of the UN committees, which will act as a quasi-judicial body tasked with evaluating whether international law has been breached in that specific case.

If you're working in big international coalitions and have the stamina for protracted advocacy efforts, the UN's different mechanisms can be used in conjunction — often together with its preeminent but highly politicized human rights body, the Human Rights Council — to really put an issue on the international agenda and propel a range of governments to address it at home. Examples include the push for accountability in Sri Lanka and the gradual but crucial recognition of equal rights for everybody regardless of their sexual orientation or gender identity.

You may also want to evaluate whether regional mechanisms such as the Inter-American or African Commissions on Human Rights can contribute to your efforts.

Finally, whatever mechanism you pursue to get the world's attention, you'll need to be prepared for your next challenge: How will you use the weight of the United Nations to push for the change you want to see on the ground?

POTENTIAL RISKS

It is vital not to skip any of the steps laid out here. Analysis and preparation are key to getting results and ensuring you don't waste energy or put yourself at further risk. Each mechanism has its own distinct way of working, so use the suggested resources to find out more and ensure you follow the correct protocols. Finally, some activists have faced threats and reprisals for having activated international mechanisms. Be sure to carry out a security analysis, take precautions, and consult the ISHR's Reprisals Handbook.

RELATED

Stop Prawer Plan » p. 78

Civil disobedience » p. 108
Jail solidarity » p. 118

Seek safety in support networks » p. 150

Pillars of power » p. 210
Spectrum of allies » p. 232

LEARN MORE

Working with the United Nations Human Rights Programme: A Handbook for Civil Society | Office of the High Commissioner for Human Rights, 2008

Directory of Human Rights Bodies | Office of the High Commissioner for Human Rights

Simple Guide to the UN Treaty Bodies | International Service for Human Rights, 2015

CHANGE A NAME TO CHANGE THE GAME

Translate complex terms into simple, everyday language, so that people can more easily discuss and confront unjust and oppressive systems.

Hellenah Okiring

The primary filter through which people understand new ideas and concepts is in the vernacular of their first language, their mother tongue. It is important, therefore, for changemakers to unpack complex theories and translate abstract, bureaucratic terms into simple, everyday language, so people can more easily identify, discuss, and confront unjust and oppressive systems.

For example, in Uganda, the term *corruption* does not have an equivalent term in any of the country's ethnic languages. The word itself is quite broad and figurative, as its Latin root means simply *to break down*. When you strip down the political meaning of corruption to its simplest form, you realize it simply means *theft*.

In a 2012 campaign against widespread misuse of public resources in Uganda, civil society organizations decided to address corruption as *theft* and corrupt officials as *thieves*. If corruption is robbery, then the corrupt are thieves — and every local language in Uganda has a word for thieves.

Anti-corruption billboard in Kayabwe, Mpigi District, Uganda. Photo: Michael Sale | CC BY-NC 2.0

The impact of this small change in the language of the campaign was phenomenal. People could suddenly understand what corruption really meant: Someone was stealing resources from everyone else, particularly from those who most needed these resources. It is easy to miss the impact of corruption when one gets lost in all the legal terms that surround this form of injustice. By calling corruption robbery, the campaign exposed the actual impacts of corruption — for example, the 16 mothers who die everyday because they can't access maternal care, the thousands of rural schools that could have been built if resources had not been stolen for private gain, the farmers who could have had access to better equipment, and the poor who could have had better healthcare, if one public official had not funnelled these resources to a personal bank account.

By changing the name of the problem, the campaign empowered everyday people to identify what was wrong and push for solutions. People knew how to deal with thieves in their communities, and now it was easy to see how they should deal with thieves in government, too. Suddenly, they were no longer powerless before an abstract injustice; the problem had local names, faces, and consequences. And once the problem was set in a more meaningful cultural context, people could more easily imagine appropriate remedies.

The response from the thieves themselves was also unprecedented. Given the embarrassment and shame that comes from being associated with an act as despicable as robbery, government officials panicked and tried to disassociate themselves from their crimes. Some guilty officials were prosecuted and had to return stolen funds. An anti-corruption bill was passed in 2013. Furthermore, the media picked up the term and began to refer to corruption as theft. The new language spread to most media outlets, who still use the term to this day.

In 2012 in Uganda, savvy campaigners changed a name and it changed the game. That was just one struggle in one country, but the principle applies around the world. What name might you change to change your game? Victory might be just one word away.

POTENTIAL RISKS

When you're using simpler language to empower your community to better understand an abstract or complex term, you run the risk of oversimplifying the issue. Oversimplifying your issue can detract from its seriousness, making you look like you are overreacting or fussing over little matters. Instead, stay focused on helping people to recognize the gravity or impact of a form of oppression or exploitation by using words in their own language that they can easily relate to. Once people have a more vivid understanding of the problem, they are empowered to better relate to its impacts and organize strategically to confront it. This applies particularly to highly sophisticated and amorphous theories that have so many forms and dimensions that it becomes easy to get lost in definitions, enabling perpetrators of injustice (and even, sometimes, our allies!) to hide behind the language they use, and blame and shame their victims into silence.

RELATED

Postcolonialism » *p. 196*

LEARN MORE

Civil Society Mourns the Uganda Lives Lost to Corruption | Black Monday Movement Newsletter, 2012

Theft of Public Resources and Lack of Proper Maternal Care | Save Woman 16, 2013

CHANGE IS THE ONLY CONSTANT

It's not just the status quo that needs to change, but the status quo inside our own heads. How can we expect to change the world without also changing how we change the world?

"Nothing endures but change."
—Heraclitus

Juman Abujbara

Activists seek justice under circumstances of tyranny, truth under circumstances of domination, and freedom under circumstances of oppression. We seek change because we deplore the status quo — but also because we recognize the need for continuous improvement. Yet, when it come to ourselves and the ways we've grown accustomed to doing things, we often enter a stage of forgetfulness about the most obvious and basic thing we know and call for: change.

Change begins with self. Not only must our social, political, environmental, and economic circumstances change, so must we be the change we want to see in the world. In order to be effective, our approaches and methods must always be reviewed, assessed, and adjusted. We must be willing to recognize and shift our own obsolete mindsets and abandon all constants. If we truly want to change the world, we must recognize that change is the only constant.

Acting from the premise that change is the only constant, you soon realize that there is not a single "right" way to engage in collective action, but rather many right ways. For change to materialize, such action must remain in a state of continuous development. This action-reflection process is an ongoing journey of learning that, like a circle, has no beginning or end *(see: PRINCIPLE: Praxis makes perfect).*

For example, when a movement or campaign is first launched, it may start with a group of five and a particular decision-making process. Over time this group becomes comfortable with their mode of operation, but when your group grows to 50 organizers, your situation will be drastically different, and you need to accept the fact that your decision-making process will need to change. This applies to many elements of campaigning, from recruitment to tactics to organization and more.

Embracing the principle that change is the only constant helps us be more open to others' feedback and ideas. Just because a new perspective is not in accord with your own, or even if it negates a deeply held belief by the larger group, this does not mean it should be discarded. On the contrary, it is in this moment that the group must pause and rethink their mindsets. Let go of your ego, be humble and appreciate others' insight and perspectives. Look for new and effective approaches to your campaign.

New beginnings are not only desirable or possible, but are as necessary as the air we breathe.

Also, just because a tactic works once, that doesn't mean we should use it over and over *(see: PRINCIPLE: Don't fall in love with your tactics)*. We should become comfortable with experimentation and the possibility of failure *(see: PRINCIPLE: Fail forward)*; only in this way will you enrich your learning and improve.

Finally, be aware of your broader context *(see: PRINCIPLE: Know your cultural terrain)* as well as your local circumstances *(see: PRINCIPLE: Know your community)*. The socio-political dynamics of our world today are vibrant and complex, requiring us to always be on the lookout, analyzing what's happening and understanding how such changes in dynamics might affect our campaigning.

POTENTIAL RISKS

When applying this principle, organizers must be conscious of three risks: tyranny of the majority, groupthink, and the hermeneutic circle. Groups characterized by groupthink and a tyranny of the majority tend to marginalize the voices that do not align with the majority. And yet it's these dissenting voices that are often the ones that offer the most insightful perspectives or that tend to avoid collectively earned disasters. (Studies have shown that groups dominated by men are particularly prone to this risk.) Groups stuck in a hermeneutic circle tend to indulge in endless theoretical discussions and feedback sessions. If the improvements, ideas, and possibilities being discussed are not applied in practice, then the discussion itself will be no more than ink on paper.

RELATED

Public narrative (story of self, us, and now) » p. 222
The onion tool » p. 238

LEARN MORE

How Diversity Makes Us Smarter
| Katherine W. Phillips, Scientific American, 2014

Pedagogy of the Oppressed | Paulo Freire

Concepts Used by Paulo Freire | Freire Institute

SEEK SAFETY IN SUPPORT NETWORKS

When activists are threatened, it's important to harness national or international networks that can provide support and deter violence.

Ben Leather

You're an activist, you want change, but powerful people are threatening violence to stop you from achieving your goals. It is vital that you put in place measures to keep you and your colleagues safe. One proven mechanism is to develop national and international support networks that can be activated at times of heightened risk, harnessing public and/or international support to deter violence against you. This is a strategy that groups like Peace Brigades International have been using to keep human rights defenders safe for over 30 years.

You need to be aware why and how you might be at risk. Whose interests are you threatening? What or who might influence the behavior of that individual or institution to deter them from hurting you or locking you up?

A volunteer member of Peace Brigade International observing a gathering. Photo: Peace Brigade International Guatemala Project

To effectively deter violence against you, you need to be able to create a political cost that those threatening you would pay if they attacked, and make sure that they are aware of that cost. What would make those people think twice before attacking you? Is it the threat of public uproar? Is it the possibility of a diplomatic sanction? Damage to their international reputation?

Based on this analysis, you can begin to assemble a support network of citizens, NGOs, journalists, embassies, politicians, or United Nations (UN) experts who are attentive to your situation, primed to take action in the case of any threats to you and your colleagues, and capable of exacting a political cost against those who might attack you. You will need to make sure your adversaries are aware of the network, its weight, and its willingness to react.

Support networks should seek to prevent as well as respond to risks. You will likely face efforts to discredit or demonize your activism, thus making you more vulnerable to attack. To avoid this, you might ask organizations in your network to take actions that will legitimize your work, either publicly, or in private with those who would do you harm. Impunity makes potential aggressors more likely to act, so ensure that your network is vigorous in demanding justice and accountability for any and all attacks.

Your potential aggressors need to understand that the world is watching and their image is at stake.

Peace Brigades International, for example, takes a very hands-on approach to creating this deterrent. When invited by threatened human rights defenders, they will arrange for international volunteers to accompany the defenders in their daily work and embody that international concern. However, this is just one way to make your support network visible. A respected newspaper may publish a story based upon an urgent action issued by an NGO, an important diplomat may meet directly with the government agency or business that opposes your demands, a solidarity caravan may visit your community, or a UN Committee may speak out about your case.

You are the best positioned to know what will really keep you safe, choosing from a range of practical and political measures. But ensure you take the time to do the analysis necessary before you start to campaign, and look for opportunities to use support networks as part of your security strategy.

POTENTIAL RISKS

Remember that your security situation is constantly evolving in response to the activities you carry out, the interests you threaten, and the victories you achieve. Don't rely upon any single strategy to keep you safe. Rather, keep analyzing and evaluating. Document any incident that might be perceived as a threat and be aware that, at some point, the only way to keep safe might be to physically relocate for a while.

RELATED

Burmese Students' Long March » p. 26
Hacking Apartheid » p. 38
Schools of Struggle » p. 60
Zapatista Caravan » p. 100

Civil disobedience » p. 108
Jail solidarity » p. 118
Subversive travel » p. 130

Activate international mechanisms » p. 138

Baltajiah (thugs) » p. 176

LEARN MORE

Unarmed Bodyguards: International Accompaniment for the Protection of Human Rights
| Liam Mahony and Luis Enrique Eguren, Kumarian Press, 1997

The Accompaniment Model in Practice
| Liam Mahoney, Fellowship of Reconciliation, 2013

The Need for Protection Networks for Women Human Rights Defenders
| Marusia López Cruz and Cristina Hardaga Fernández, ISHR, 2015

SHAME THE AUTHORITIES BY DOING THEIR JOB

Fix a problem as best you can in order to pressure authorities to fix it properly.

> ***"Egg whites are good for a lot of things — lemon meringue pie, angel food cake, and clogging up radiators."***
> *—MacGyver*

Gui Bueno

Imagine a problem that you, as a regular citizen, can't solve alone. Let's say your city had decided to privatize road repair, and now your street, paved with poor materials, has lots of potholes. You could complain about it, you could create a petition to pressure local authorities and the paving company, or you could stand idly by waiting for someone else to take action.

Or . . . you could choose to fix it yourself! Of course, there's a huge gap in quality between what you and your friends can do with a limited amount of time, money, and expertise, and what a professional fix would look like. But if you fill the potholes temporarily with cement, traffic would immediately move better and you could use the action to gather support and build pressure against the privatization of public services. It's a great trick: temporarily solving a problem with a quick, little fix that can build support for bigger and better solutions. You could even put a sign on

Sign memorializing the street where members of the Black Panther Party escorted children through a busy intersection in Oakland, CA, until the authorities installed a traffic light a year ahead of schedule. Photo: Eric Fischer | CC BY 2.0

each patched-up pothole saying "citizens, not politicians, fixed this mess." It might just embarrass the city administration into living up to its responsibility to provide public services.

The Black Panther Party made excellent use of this tactic in the 1960s. Sick of waiting for the City of Oakland to install a traffic light at a busy intersection near a school where several children had been killed and injured by vehicles, the Panthers set up an armed crossing guard to escort children across the intersection. No further deaths or injuries were reported until the traffic light was finally installed — more than a year ahead of schedule.

In another, more recent, example, the Rolling Jubilee campaign bought off hundreds of thousands of dollars worth of average Americans' bad debts for pennies on the dollar, and then forgave that debt. While the project does indeed help a few people facing bankruptcy, it was never conceived as a silver bullet for people's debt problems at large. Of equal or greater importance was the message it sent about the arbitrary and unfair nature of the entire banking system. It's an ad hoc fix that underscores just how broken the entire banking system is, and how easy and beneficial it would be to simply erase that crippling debt.

Similarly, in a city such as São Paulo, Brazil, which has no recycling policies, citizens can't create selective garbage collection by themselves, but they can bring visibility and respect to the informal workers that make their living — and take care of 90 percent of São Paulo's recycling — through their own DIY solution *(see: STORY: Pimp My . . . Carroça!)*. What society can do is celebrate them as heroes, improve their work conditions, and galvanize support for city-wide recycling and trash collection.

Or take the Max Feffer tunnel in São Paulo, whose walls were totally covered by grime and soot from engine exhaust. Alexandre Orion chose to selectively clean some parts of it through reverse graffiti — erasing some of the soot to expose the

wall beneath, rather than drawing over it. No police officer could ever arrest him for cleaning a public space, so local authorities had no choice but to clean all the walls in the tunnel, which is what Orion wanted in the first place!

When citizens are able to fix something completely, but opt only for an ad hoc DIY solution, that's bad. But an ad hoc solution can be used as a provocative first step towards bolder and more lasting solutions *(see: PRINCIPLE: Escalate strategically)*. All it takes to devise a clever, unconventional solution that will attract attention to your cause, and pressure the authorities into action, is a little creativity and a willingness to get your hands dirty.

The graffiti artist Alexandre Orion started and the city's administration finished the work of cleaning a tunnel in São Paulo, Brazil. Photo: Alexandre Orion

POTENTIAL RISKS

1. Remember: this is all about temporary solutions. So, be clear to keep the focus on the actual, lasting change that you are fighting for. You don't want your ad hoc solution to let the authorities off the hook from fulfilling their responsibilities.
2. Don't make a DIY fix that could break and hurt someone. D'oh! *(see: PRINCIPLE: Take risks but take care)*
3. Be clear about whether you want to make a temporary fix, or fix the problem for real. Sometimes what you actually want is to have the community solve its own problems in a way the state never could.

RELATED

Replacing Cops with Mimes » p. 54
Schools of Struggle » p. 60

LEARN MORE

Strike Debt — Debt Resistance for the 99%!

Rolling Jubilee

Rolling Jubilee Is a Spark, Not the Solution | Andrew Ross and Astra Taylor, The Nation, 2012

Alexandre Orion's Photostream | Flickr

Daycare Center Sit-In | Beautiful Trouble

USE HUMOR TO UNDERMINE AUTHORITY

Especially when the powerful rule through fear and intimidation, humor, laughter, and absurdity can be powerful tools for undermining power and emboldening people to stand up for their rights.

"The human race has only one really effective weapon and that is laughter."
—Mark Twain

Elspeth Tilley

Humor has been used throughout history to give hope to the subjugated, rile oppressors, and encourage resistance. It can be a powerful weapon, psychologically cutting an oppressor down to size and undermining their social legitimacy — no wonder anti-Nazi jokes were banned during the Third Reich. Humor can also nourish resistance, showing that despite bitter odds, the spirit is unbreakable — hence Antonin Obrdlik's observation, "gallows humor is an index of strength . . . on the part of oppressed peoples."[1]

Sigmund Freud identified three kinds of humor: *body humor, mind humor*, and *spirit humor*. All three can be used to undermine power and buoy the spirits of the oppressed.

Bodies are funny because they are uncontrollable: Even the powerful fart, hiccup, and fall, and we can subvert their authority by pointing that out. Pictures of

1 Antonin J. Obrdlik, " 'Gallows Humor' — A Sociological Phenomenon," *American Journal of Sociology* 47, no. 5 (1942): 709-716, http://www.jstor.org/stable/2769536.

Zimbabwean President Robert Mugabe tripping went viral on the internet, and his futile efforts to control the situation by demanding photographers delete images that had already gone worldwide only fueled the hilarity. Seeing the powerful try and fail to wield absolute control makes us laugh.

Mind humor is useful when freedom of speech is restricted, or direct confrontation with authority is made illegal. Satire, irony, wordplay, puns, and double entendre can communicate at multiple levels, subtly signalling an insult or joke to one audience but being difficult to pin down as offensive or illegal by those in power (and thus difficult to punish). Plus, we laugh with pleasure at the sheer cleverness of a creative wordplay. The subversive power of such forms of humor was on full display in a recent decision by Chinese officials to ban puns and wordplay in news media.

Spirit humor, finally, refers to our joy in seeing an underdog triumph, particularly if they use the oppressor's own weapon against them. A great example of this is Anna Gensler's Instagram art project Instagranniepants. Tired of being the victim of online sexual harassment, Gensler started incorporating the harassing messages she received into funny naked caricatures she drew of the harassers, and posting the results online, where they quickly became a popular comic meme.

Bassem Youssef, known as the Jon Stewart of Egypt, had his satirical television show cancelled in 2013 and was forced to flee the country, though his example lives on in Cairo's political graffiti. Photo: Gigi Ibrahim | CC BY 2.0

Troublemaking figures like the trickster, fool, and clown can also be used to unsettle authority figures and reclaim a sense of agency in the face of suffocating institutional strictures. Tricksters have a long tradition of ignoring social rules, mischievously deceiving authority figures, and turning serious activities into fun. Their position outside the expectations of "normal" society means they can flip oppression simply by playfully refusing its mechanisms of control, and often they can express ideas others are afraid to voice.

Effective humor delivers the audience the justice they crave, so setting up the premise of a superior or conceited character on a pedestal, who is then fodder for the "fool" to disrupt, is important. The pleasure that people experience witnessing a disruption of power they aren't sure they can achieve themselves can either be a release valve, providing the only safe way to defy authority, or serve as a model, motivating the public to seek justice in the real world.

The Clandestine Insurgent Rebel Clown Army (CIRCA) is a great contemporary example of trickster humor in action. CIRCA has shown up at protest marches throughout Europe to undermine the macho posturing of police (as well as some of the more aggro protesters) and generally add a carnivalesque, anti-authoritarian atmosphere. At an anti-war protest at a UK army recruitment office, for example, CIRCA members used feather dusters to "clean" soldiers and police cars, and clever mimicry to parrot officers' walks and gestures, leaving even the officers struggling not to laugh. Once police had removed them from the building, the recruitment office closed early, so the clowns put a "sign up here" table outside the door and began signing people up to the clown army, instead of the regular army.

Finally, we're more likely to remember something — and share it — if it makes us laugh. We are hardwired to be more likely to post something funny on social media than something newsy and informative. "Social Justice Comedian" Negin Farsad's comic ads satirizing Muslim stereotypes went viral on the internet, garnering hundreds of thousands of views. (See the whole story of the campaign in the 2012 comedy documentary *The Muslims Are Coming!*)

It is a core premise of the Clandestine Insurgent Rebel Clown Army that mocking and utterly confusing the enemy can be more powerful than direct confrontation. Photo: CIRCA

continued on next page ›

POTENTIAL RISKS

If taking aim at a real person, be sure that a reasonable bystander would recognize your material as clearly satirical, rather than mistake it for actual facts that could be considered defamatory. Turkish President Recep Tayyip Erdogan tried in 2016 to have German poet Jan Böhmermann prosecuted over a satirical poem, but German prosecutors called the poem "characteristic of the art form of satire and caricature" due to its characteristics of "exaggeration, distortion, and disassociation," and refused to press charges.

Secondly, humor is very time and place specific. It often does not cross cultures well, and even within a cultural group there will be distinct subgroups with shifting understandings of what is socially acceptable, so it's essential to know your audience *(see: PRINCIPLE: Consider your audience)*. One of the best ways to reduce this risk is to bring in diverse voices, incorporate members of your intended audience into your creative team, and get lots of feedback on your work as you develop it.

Thirdly, being the butt of a joke can hurt. If you are already vulnerable, it can be devastating. Use humor to redress power imbalances, not exacerbate them: "punch up," not down.

A final risk comes when those with power harness the guise of a trickster, playing at irreverence or setting themselves up as a maverick, even though they are actually part of the establishment. It is tough to successfully satirize a figure who has already styled themselves as a parody of or disrupter to authority, however artificial that facade may be. In that circumstance, responding with humor probably won't work, and you may need to focus on exposing the extent of the target's actual authority and control through rational information. (Once the extent of their privilege is clearly re-established, humor might again be effective. Remember, anti-authoritarian humor is about justly disrupting hierarchies, so your audience first needs to clearly see the hierarchy that's there.)

RELATED

Replacing Cops with Mimes » *p. 54*
Yellow Pigs in Parliament » *p. 96*

Civil disobedience » *p. 108*
Music video » *p. 124*

LEARN MORE

Humour in Political Activism
| Majken Sørensen, Palgrave MacMillan, 2016

Serious Play: Modern Clown Performance
| Louise Peacock, Intellect Books, 2009

And Then, You Act: Making Art in an Unpredictable World
| Anne Bogart, Taylor and Francis, 2007

Colbert's America: Satire and Democracy
| Sophia A. McClennen, Springer, 2011

WOULD YOU LIKE SOME STRUCTURE WITH YOUR MOMENTUM?

Success comes from incorporating the strengths of both mass protests and structure-based organizing — so that outbreaks of widespread revolt complement long-term organizing.

"You don't organize movements; you build organizations, and if movements emerge, you may catch their energy and grow. Occupy Wall Street moved the ball farther in three months than a lot of us did in three decades."

—Danny Cantor

Mark Engler and Paul Engler

Over time, a gulf has emerged between two different approaches to creating social change.

Organizers in the labor movement and in community-based organizations typically focus on person-by-person recruitment, careful leadership development, and the creation of stable institutional bodies that can leverage the power of their members over time. As an organizing tradition, this approach can be described as one based on *structure*.

Protester in Hong Kong's 2014 "Umbrella Movement" stands defiantly as teargas wafts through the streets. Photo: Pasu Au Yeung | CC BY-SA

In contrast, broad-based revolts like those that rocked the world in 2011 were marked by unruly and widespread disobedience, undertaken outside the confines of any formal organization. This approach emphasizes the disruptive power of mass mobilizations that coalesce quickly, draw in participants not previously involved in organizing, and leave elites scrambling to adjust to a new political landscape. This tradition can be dubbed *mass protest*.

The divide between *structure* and *mass protest* or between long-term organization and disruptive uprisings, runs deep through social movement history. It's not that one of these approaches is right and the other wrong; both have their strengths and weaknesses. The trick for organizers is to figure out how their strengths can be used in tandem — so that long-term organizing and outbreaks of widespread revolt build off one another.

Unfortunately, there's often distrust in both directions that must first be overcome. Advocates of mass protest are wary of the transactional politics of structure-based organizing and the tactical accommodations with power-holders that such politics tend to promote. They wonder how even a long string of incremental victories will ever add up to any meaningful change in the rules of the game. Meanwhile, structure-based organizers are typically wary of movement mobilizations because disruptive power is hard to understand and even harder to direct. Can outbreaks of mass defiance really be intentionally triggered and magnified? If so, how, exactly?

Fortunately, the world of social movement thinking is now experiencing a renaissance on this front, with traditions of strategic nonviolence providing critical practical insights into how to orchestrate disruptive protest. It's not just about ripe or unripe *conditions* over which organizers have little control, but about the *skills* organizers can bring to help shape mass mobilization. These skills include the ability to recognize when the terrain for protest is fertile, the talent for staging creative and provocative acts of civil disobedience, the capacity for intelligently escalating *(see: PRINCIPLE: Escalate strategically)* once a mobilization is under way, and the foresight to make sure that short-term cycles of disruption contribute to furthering longer-term goals.

Many new activists are drawn into politics through the energy of a mass mobilization but are disappointed when these movements suddenly decline, as they inevitably do. The challenge here is how to combine explosive short-term uprisings with long-term organizing to make movements more sustainable. Coming from the opposite perspective, veteran community organizers who have recently experienced the tremendous momentum that disruptive outbreaks can generate — even if much of it is fleeting — have been willing to reconsider their focus on organizations at the expense of movements.

A focus on mass protest need not deny the importance of building organizational structures, just as an appreciation of structure does not preclude support for widespread mobilization during periods of peak activity. An organizing model that integrates the two asks: *What can organizers do to maximize the long-term impact of disruptive power?*

RELATED

Honk at Parliament » p. 44
Schools of Struggle » p. 60
Stop Prawer Plan » p. 78

Civil disobedience » p. 108

Al faza'a (a surge of solidarity) » p. 172
The NGO-ization of resistance » p. 200

Pillars of power » p. 210
Spectrum of allies » p. 232

LEARN MORE

This is an Uprising: How Nonviolent Revolt is Shaping the 21st Century | ThisIsAnUprising.org, 2016

Dan Cantor's Machine | The American Prospect, January/February 2014

Movement Net Lab

THEORIES

Big-picture ideas that help us understand how the world works and how we might change it.

"There's nothing so practical as a good theory."
—George Lakey

Ever wished someone would take the most important ideas from revolutionary thinkers like Paulo Freire, Arundhati Roy, and Antonio Gramsci, and cook them down into fierce, accessible nuggets of theory, tailored to the pragmatic needs of the everyday troublemaker? Look no further.

○ ○ ○ ○

AL FAZA'A (A SURGE OF SOLIDARITY)

A key segment of your supporters will only join at peak moments of your campaign — usually in response to an external event — and then disappear again. To win, you must be ready to make the most of this surge.

Origins: *Faza'a* is a Bedouin term that means solidarity, and refers to when other tribes are called upon for help in wartime or on a specific occasion. It conveys the idea of taking rapid and imminent action to help people in danger.

> ***"Beware the level-headed person if they're angry."***
> *—Arabic proverb*

Safa' Al Jayoussi

Most people do not feel the need to act in circumstances they see as normal. However, a specific event — a brave act of resistance; or a disputed election, corruption scandal, or police beating — can serve as an emotional trigger, moving people to respond en masse and join actions to address the problem. They come in large numbers, with new ideas and energy, and boost your campaign for a brief while. These moments are often amplified by media, particularly social media, as trending topics generate even more attention and interest in the campaign. People's enthusiasm is often momentary, however, which can make it difficult to retain their support once the external element of emergency that drew them to act recedes.

An example of this phenomenon is Greenpeace's "Jordan Is Not Nuclear" campaign, which sought to stop the construction of a nuclear facility in Jordan in 2011. The number of people who were active in the campaign prior to the Fukushima disaster of 2011, which saw the partial meltdown of a nuclear reactor in Japan following a major earthquake and tidal wave, was very small compared to the number of people who were inspired to act immediately following the disaster. Thirty thousand Jordanians, including many Jordanian tribes, joined the movement in the aftermath of the disaster. They joined *al faza'a (a surge of solidarity)* to save their country out of fear that a similar nuclear disaster might befall them if the facility were built.

There are many other examples in recent history, including the public outcry at the 2012 gang rape in Delhi, the mass outrage after the self-immolation of the Tunisian street vendor that sparked that country's revolution and set off the Arab Spring, the Occupy Wall Street movement in the US, and so many others.

Al faza'a, in its traditional sense, is perceived as a positive trait among Arabs because it implies solidarity and friendship. Nonetheless, it presents challenges to modern campaigns because the vast majority of supporters are drawn by external events, and therefore may not share the strategic vision or values of your campaign.

In a moment of anger sparked by the self-immolation of street vendor Mohamed Bouazizi, hundreds of thousands of Tunisians united against the regime and took to the streets in mass protests, eventually ousting decades-long dictator Ben Ali.

The key is to know what to expect and to make the most of the skills and talents that are suddenly available to you.

Lifted by a huge surge of support, you can transform your campaign from a specialist discussion going on behind closed doors among a small number of activists into a matter of public opinion *(see: STORY: Stolen Gas Campaign p. 72)*. Use your strength of numbers to shift the balance of power and pressure decision makers to heed your demands. Also, seize the opportunity to identify potential leaders and activists and recruit them to your campaign.

Eventually, the surge dissipates, so it's wise to set your expectations early on. Instead of being disappointed when the momentum wanes, take advantage of the opportunity to build connections with those who have specific skills or networks that may support you later on *(see: PRINCIPLE: Would you like some structure with your momentum? p. 166)*.

Taiwanese students take part in a mass protest as part of the Sunflower Student Movement in 2014. Photo: Artemas Liu | CC BY 2.0

RELATED

Battle of the Camel » p. 14
Burmese Students' Long March » p. 26
Honk at Parliament » p. 44
Stolen Gas Campaign » p. 72
Stop Prawer Plan » p. 78
Welcome to Palestine » p. 90

Would you like some structure with your momentum? » p. 166

The Global South » p. 188

Art of Hosting » p. 206
Pillars of power » p. 210
Spectrum of allies » p. 232

LEARN MORE

Arab Spring: A Research and Study Guide
| Cornell University Library, 2011

Solidarity with the Palestinian Popular Resistance
| Mondoweiss, 2015

Occupy Wall Street

○ ○ ○ ○

BALTAJIAH (THUGS)

A common political formation shows up across the Arab World: an often marginalized grouping of individuals that the government can call on to momentarily disrupt movements seeking change.

Origins: The word originates from the Turkish language where a *baltaji* was a person who walked with the army to clear a way through the woods and build forts using an axe (the *balta*). The term then took a different meaning when about 300 years ago in the Ottoman Empire (modern-day Turkey), violent pro-regime thugs acted on behalf of the authorities to force hungry protesters to stop protesting.

"And so now, . . . [the despot] collects 10,000 loafers who are to impersonate the people as Snug the Joiner does the lion."
—Karl Marx

Ahmad Kassawneh

Across the Middle East and North Africa, tribes often maintain loyalty and close ties to protect themselves from oppression. The state cunningly takes advantage of this defense-mechanism dynamic to transform blind loyalty into an instrument of oppression they can use for their own purposes.

Baltajiah, which is derived from the Arabic word *balta* meaning axe, is the name Egyptians give to pro-regime supporters used by the state to uphold its apparatus.

In other countries they are called different names. In Syria: *shabiha*, which is derived from the word *shabah*, meaning ghost, because the thugs dress as normal civilians and emerge anonymously from within the crowd to cause a disruption. In Jordan and Palestine: *sahijieh*, from the root word *sahja*, or clapping, originating from a type of bedouin dance, and referring to the act of mindlessly applauding the regime despite its faults.

These groups can be manipulated to take advantage of the internal conflicts and social divisions among different ideologies, religions, and sects within a society. They are mostly unorganized and marginalized, and come together temporarily to disrupt people seeking change. In turn, they are supported and empowered by the state, and thus become its blind followers regardless of its merit or broader legitimacy.

In some countries, the state rewards such groups with monetary and non-monetary benefits in order to maintain their loyalty and to be able to mobilize them as they wish. The thugs are particularly useful to these governments,

Graffiti in Cairo reads "Police are the baltajiah," making the point that the thugs do the dirty work of the regime. Photo: Hossam al-Hamalawy / CC BY-NC-SA 2.0

because it's a way for them to use force and violence to disrupt change and deter activism without being held accountable by the broader society, the international community, human rights organizations, or other relevant bodies. (The crimes, after all, were committed by the baltajiah, not by anyone in a government uniform.)

The widespread use of these groups was starkly evident in the way states responded to the uprisings that swept the Arab world in 2011. Regime after regime used thugs to deter, or at least attempt to deter, people from joining the protests. But under the hot glare of media coverage (especially social media), the tactic backfired, instead increasing sympathy for the protesters and drawing yet more people into the streets. This was most true in Egypt and Tunisia. Unfortunately, however, things turned out quite differently in Syria, where the violence of the state proved stronger than the power of free speech, leading to civil war, or in Jordan, where the state successfully used thugs and other tactics to dissolve the popular movement.

Activists in the Middle East/North Africa region need to be aware of how the state uses thugs as an instrument of control; we need to better understand the risks, develop preemptive strategies to confront and disarm them (literally or figuratively), and learn how to spot thugs and avoid colliding with them. By understanding the motives of baltajiah and strategizing ways to engage their hearts and minds with our kindness and creativity, we might compel them to rethink their blind obedience, and neutralize their worst tendencies. Furthermore, if the tactic backfires on the state, we should be ready to take advantage of that moment by mobilizing people who share our principles but are not yet active in our campaign *(see: METHODOLOGY: Spectrum of allies p. 232)*.

RELATED

Battle of the Camel » *p. 14*

Seek safety in support networks » *p. 150*

Pillars of power » *p. 210*
Spectrum of allies » *p. 232*

LEARN MORE

Baltajiah | Information International, 2011

Shabiha | Wikipedia

This Is Just a Warning: Pro-Regime Gunmen Break Syrian Cartoonist's Hands | The Star, 2011

Pro-Regime Thugs Attack Hong Kong Protesters | Socialist Alternative

Jordan Revolt Renewed | Socialist Review, 2012

"DEMOCRACY PROMOTION"

Democracy promotion **is the term the US uses to describe efforts to penetrate and control emergent civil societies in targeted countries — those with regimes deemed unfriendly or unstable by policymakers.**

Origins: Began in the 1980s, expanded with the collapse of the Soviet block and the spread of the so-called color revolutions.

"This is not democracy. It is to politics what McDonald's is to food."
—John Pilger

George Katsiaficas

In the 1980s, as People Power revolts across Asia transformed political dynamics, US global strategy changed from sole reliance on repressive military interventions and covert CIA actions to include a public component called "democracy promotion," the attempt to penetrate and control emergent civil societies in targeted countries (those with regimes deemed unfriendly or unstable by American policymakers). Tens of millions of US dollars were poured into programs formerly managed by the CIA, such as creating "friendly" trade unions, political parties, feminist alliances, activist clusters, and media that would support US transnational interests. In combination with the National Endowment for Democracy, the AFL-CIO, the

A mural in Caracas, Venezuela, shows Che Guevara, Simón Bolivar, and Hugo Chavez knocking out Uncle Sam, capitalism, and imperialism. Photo: Alexandre Haubrich | CC BY-NC 2.0

international committees of the Democratic and Republican parties, and the US Chamber of Commerce, NGOs chosen by US officials were funded with the aim of building friendly voices within emergent civil societies in order to channel them into transnational alliances with global elites.

Often this effort required undermining indigenous radical formations that organically developed through struggles against US-backed dictatorships — as in the Philippines under Marcos or more recently in Egypt before the overthrow of Mubarak. The goal in both these cases was to suppress popular demands that arose from below. American policymakers are well aware that the radical impetus in the streets, if left to develop according to its own logic, could well continue to expand and become a threat to both US strategic military interests and corporate domination. US infiltration of indigenous civil society groups is often a preventative measure meant precisely to undermine movements' radical potential. As James Petras observed during the Arab Spring, "The risk of waiting too long, of sticking with the dictator, is that the uprising radicalizes: The ensuing change sweeps away both the regime and the state apparatus, turning a political uprising into a social revolution." (In cases where entrenched regimes unfriendly to the United States cannot be overthrown through military intervention, such as Milošević in Yugoslavia, strategic nonviolent opposition led by NGOs was used as an alternative tactic.)

Excerpted from George Katsiaficas, Asia's Unknown Uprisings, Vol. II: People Power in the Philippines, Burma, Tibet, China, Taiwan, Bangladesh, Nepal, Thailand and Indonesia, 1947-2009. *PM Press, 2013, by permission.*

RELATED

○ ○ ○ ○

Neoliberalism » *p. 192*

Postcolonialism » *p. 196*

The Global South » *p. 188*

The NGO-ization of resistance » *p. 200*

LEARN MORE

Oligarchs, Demagogues, and Mass Revolts Against Democracy | James Petras, Dissident Voice, 2013

Killing Hope: US Military and CIA Interventions Since World War II | William Blum, Common Courage Press, 2004

The Iranian Revolution of 1979, which saw the overthrow of a pro-American dynasty, helped galvanize American policymakers to pursue a policy of infiltrating and co-opting civil society groups to undermine their revolutionary potential. Photo: Aristotle Saris

O O O O

FEMINISM

Feminist social movements identify patriarchal power as a fundamental source of injustice and inequality, and hence call to transform gender power relations in all domains.

Origins: Though the history of feminism tends to be divided into phases or "waves" starting in the 19th century, movements for women's rights and gender equality stretch back much further, manifesting in many different ways across different cultures.

"I am not free while any woman is unfree, even when her shackles are very different from my own."
—Audre Lorde

Rudo Chigudu

In thinking about feminism, it is essential to start neither from fear nor fantasy. While fear stems from the belief that feminism is anti-male, fantasy is the belief that feminism is easily attainable.

Feminism is a social movement that challenges a system of sexist oppression — called patriarchy — that is deeply entrenched in many societies and into which we are all born. Feminism aims to eliminate all forms of discrimination against women, including those related to sex and gender as well as class, race, ethnicity, ability,

In the Rojava region of Syria, women participate on an equal footing with men at every level and also organize in autonomous councils, assemblies, and committees, to address their specific concerns. Photo: Kurdishstruggle | CC BY 2.0

sexual orientation, and other forms of exclusion. This movement of resistance is often met with violence, stigmatization, and condemnation because it seeks to deconstruct an oppressive power structure, thereby challenging those that benefit from it.

The story of the Miniskirt March is a clear manifestation of this theory in action *(see: STORY: Miniskirt March p. 50)*. In response to recurrent incidents of violence, harassment, and stigmatization against women's choice of clothing, women and human rights activists organized a march wearing miniskirts and tight-fitting clothes and paraded the streets of Harare in protest. Although the march was met with mixed reactions from the general public, it disrupted an otherwise banal power structure.

Feminisms are diverse in origin and expression. Generally, though, they analyze and challenge patriarchal power as well as other systems of privilege and subordination. Feminisms have evolved over time from making linkages between slavery and women's bondage to focusing on women's subordination in the private sphere, including matters such as bodily autonomy, sexuality, and gender-based violence. In more recent times feminism has become more expansive, involving greater diversity across generations, classes, ethnicities, and sexual orientations.

Given that the vast majority of people are born into a world full of bias, be it gender, class, race, or nationality, we have all been largely shaped by patriarchy and often play into it in unconscious ways. Feminism seeks to create a critical political consciousness that enables people to identify injustices and challenge them. In this sense, challenging patriarchy involves challenging our privileges, our prejudices, and ourselves. Thus, we should always be sure that our gender-consciousness — our efforts to challenge the implicit oppression within us — becomes a way of seeing and living, and is implemented in other struggles for social change *(see: PRINCIPLE: Challenge patriarchy as you organize)*.

Feminism is not something one is born into; it is a political act and a choice to be feminist. This choice is then manifested through one's actions. The success of feminist organizing in challenging complex systems of power thrives on creating an environment where revolutionary feminist consciousness can be cultivated, without reproducing the same problems that dominant systems create to begin with *(see: THEORY: Anti-oppression)*.

The goal of feminist organizing is for all people, regardless of their gender or their sexuality, to live fully as who they are in a world that is peaceful and abundant with possibilities.

Feminism is about recognizing that all oppressions intersect. As Audre Lorde says, "I am not free while any woman is unfree, even when her shackles are very different from my own."

RELATED

Boxing Gender Oppression » p. 20
Miniskirt March » p. 50

Public narrative (story of self, us, and now) » p. 222

LEARN MORE

We Should All Be Feminists | TEDxTalk, Chimamanda Ngozi Adichie, 2013

We Should All Be Feminists | Chimamanda Ngozi Adichie, 2014

○ ○ ○ ○

THE GLOBAL SOUTH

The Global South is not a place, but a way of talking about a diverse set of struggles: the uprising of the planet's people against neoliberal policies, at least, and against the capitalist system, at most.

Origins: The Global South emerged as a full-blown category in the 1980s, the final decade of the Cold War, when the Third World project had largely vanished and the Global South came forward as its inchoate successor.

"But down here, down
near the roots
is where memory
omits no memory
and here are those
who defy death for
and die for
and thus together achieve
what was impossible
that the whole world
would know
that the South,
that the South also exists."
—Mario Benedetti,
"El Sur también existe."

Vijay Prashad

The Global South is not a place.

In response to the neoliberal attack on the social world of the world's poor from the late 1970s onwards, protests broke out from Caracas (1989) to Seattle (1999). These protests heralded the slogan *Another World is Possible*. The term *Global South*, used in different forums with various degrees of urgency, referred to the demands of these protests to end the theft of the commons, the theft of human dignity and rights, and the undermining of democratic institutions and the promises of modernity. It is the name for the protests against neoliberal policies that produce an unequal world.

What are these policies? Pushed by the IMF and the World Bank, these policies used the Third World debt crisis and the problem of insufficient municipal revenue in the former colonies of Asia, Africa, and the Americas to push for cuts to social services, a transfer of social wealth to the private sector, and the forcing open of vast areas of human life to the commodity process. Water was no longer to be a common resource, but would be owned, bottled, and sold. Education became a commodity, not a right. So did health care. Conditions of life for the world's billions deteriorated. The end result: Five multi-billionaires now own as much as half the world's entire population (3.8 billion people). That obscenity is what has resulted in a massive, world-wide challenge arising under the banner of the *Global South*.

The Global South is this: a world of protest, a whirlwind of creative activity. These protests have produced an opening that has no easily definable political direction. Some of them turn backwards, taking refuge in imagined unities of the past or in the divine realm. Others are merely defensive, seeking to survive in the present. And yet others find the present intolerable and nudge the world toward the future.

G8 summit protest skit dramatizing the power imbalance underlying global trade negotiations, 2007. Photo: turbotorbs / CC BY-NC 2.0

RELATED

○ ○ ○ ○

Jorge González Camarena's 300-square-meter mural "Presence of Latin America," located in the Casa del Arte, Universidad de Concepción, Chile. Photo: Farisori | CC BY-SA 3.0

LEARN MORE

The Poorer Nations: A Possible History of the Global South | Vijay Prashad, Verso, 2013

Polarizing Development: Alternatives to Neoliberalism and the Crisis | Lucia Pradella and Thomas Marois, Pluto, 2014

○ ○ ○ ○

NEOLIBERALISM

Neoliberalism, today's dominant ideology, reduces the state to a handmaiden of transnational capital. In pursuing the relentless privatization of the commons, its policies inevitably spark popular discontent.

Origins: *Liberalism* was the economic philosophy of laissez-faire capitalism that emerged in the 1870s. Almost 100 years later, *neoliberalism* emerged as a set of global policies implemented by the right-wing governments of Margaret Thatcher in the UK and Ronald Reagan in the US. The theoretical foundations were provided by Milton Friedman and the Chicago School of economists.

"The neoliberal project [is] not an economic project at all, but a political project, designed to devastate the imagination, and willing . . . to destroy the capitalist order itself if that's what it took to make it seem inevitable."
—David Graeber

Firoze Manji

We are living through a period of unprecedented concentration and centralization of capital on a global scale, with a few hundred transnational corporations controlling almost every aspect of our economies. Capitalists have responded to the falling rate of profit in production by increasingly speculating in credit, property, and stock markets — the unproductive sectors of the economy. Under such conditions, accumulation by dispossession becomes the order of the day: privatizing public services and selling off state assets; eliminating jobs and suppressing wages; extracting natural resources; forcing open territories for exploitation. All of this results in governments being more accountable to corporations, banks, and financial institutions than they are to citizens — a political dispossession that only compounds the social and economic dispossession. This phenomenon has come to be known as *neoliberalism.*

Neoliberalism, in a word, is the attempt of capital to resolve its crises by subjecting all aspects of life, from health and education to arts, livelihoods, and democracy itself, to the ideology of the free market. When implemented in advanced capitalist countries, neoliberalism is referred to as "austerity measures," whereas for Third World populations it has been called "structural adjustment" or, more recently, "poverty reduction strategy papers" (PRSPs).

Beyond differences in naming, a common set of destructive social and economic policies are implemented in countries around the globe, privatizing and deregulating economies for the benefit of a few people with political and economic power. The state is declared inefficient and public services are first allowed to deteriorate from lack of funding before being sold off cheaply to the private sector, principally to transnational corporations. The state is prohibited from investing in social infrastructure, including health, education, transport, and telecommunications, which are instead managed by corporations, for profit. In the

"Sorry, the lifestyle you ordered is out of stock": Graffiti artist Banksy illustrates the limits of the neoliberal mindset. Photo: KiyoTomo Mickey Monkichi

Third World, the state is barred from subsidizing agricultural production (unlike in Europe and the US). Tariff barriers protecting national economies are removed, rights to natural resources are auctioned off cheaply, and taxes are cut, resulting in ballooning wealth inequality and growing public debt.

Notably, as the state recedes, public services that corporations are unable to make profits from, such as primary education in poor communities, begin to be provided in part by charitable NGOs, another face of the private sector that is ultimately not accountable to citizens. The result is that the essentials of life that everyone has rights to — health care, education, water, etc. — are now selectively offered as charity.[1]

Fortunately, there *are* alternatives. The destruction caused by neoliberal policies has resulted in a growing crisis of credibility in capitalism's ability to deliver on its promises, and growing movements demand a new approach, including the Tunisian and Egyptian revolutions, the Occupy movements, as well as protest movements across the African continent,[2] Spain, and Greece. For the first time in decades, there is now an appreciation of the material basis for solidarity across the globe based on a shared sense of discontent at the ruin that neoliberalism is making of all that we value.

1 As Arundhati Roy observes: "NGOs give the *impression* that they are filling the vacuum created by a retreating state. And they are, but in a materially inconsequential way. Their *real* contribution is that they defuse political anger and dole out as aid or benevolence what people ought to have by right" (Arundhati Roy, *The End of Imagination*, Chicago: Haymarket Books, 2016).

2 Firoze Manji, "African Awakening: The Courage to Invent the Future," in *African Awakening: The Emerging Revolutions*, ed. Firoze Manji and Sokari Ekine (Oxford: Pambazuka Press, 2012).

RELATED

Schools of Struggle » p. 60
Zapatista Caravan » p. 100

"Democracy promotion" » p. 180
The Global South » p. 188
The NGO-ization of resistance » p. 200

Pillars of power » p. 210
Spectrum of allies » p. 232

LEARN MORE

A Brief History of Neoliberalism
| David Harvey, Oxford University Press, 2007

The Shock Doctrine: The Rise of Disaster Capitalism
| Naomi Klein, Knopf Canada, 2007

Ending the Crisis of Capitalism or Ending Capitalism
| Samir Amin, Fahamu Books, 2010

Structural Adjustment Explained
| Martin Khor, Global Issues, 2005

Structural Adjustment: The Policy Roots of Economic Crisis, Poverty, and Inequality (The SAPRI Report)
| The Structural Adjustment Participatory Review International Network (SAPRIN), Zed Books, 2004

Austerity: The History of a Dangerous Idea
| Mark Blyth, Talks at Google, 2013

○ ○ ○ ○

POSTCOLONIALISM

Postcolonial theory forces us to acknowledge that oppression occurs not just in economic relations, but also in the very categories of meaning-making that produce reality as we know, understand, and live it.

Origins: Heavily indebted to Michel Foucault's archaeological approach to discourse, Antonio Gramsci's work on the subaltern, and Frantz Fanon's psychoanalysis of racial discrimination and colonialism, postcolonial theory emerged from the Subaltern Studies Group in the mid-1980s — a group of scholars mostly comprised of Indian historians and/or Marxists.

"Imperialism leaves behind germs of rot which we must clinically detect and remove from our land but from our minds as well."
—Frantz Fanon

Ram Bhat

Activism too often relies on a black-and-white narrative that neatly divides the world between oppressor and oppressed. As a result, activists often lean on a universalist language of human rights, democracy, and justice to fight back. Postcolonial theory, however, recognizes that any discourse is historically rooted in a particular ideological framework. While postcolonial theory is sympathetic to the aims and intentions of activism, it also complicates the allegedly universalist discourses that activism tends to rely on.

Postcolonialism is useful for activists who want to reflect on the historical roots of their discourse and the unintended consequences of using their discourse on behalf of people of the so-called Third World. It creates a discursive space where subaltern context and agency are rendered visible and capable of speaking to power. Indeed, it profoundly transforms our notions of where power is located in our struggles. It forces us to acknowledge that oppression occurs not just in economic relations, but also in the very categories of meaning-making that produce reality as we know, understand, and live it.

Postcolonial theory moves away from a strictly materialist analysis, preferring instead to go with a Foucaultian perspective; namely, that it is discourse that produces reality. This is not to deny that there is a material reality out there. Rather, it posits that every material reality "out there" can only be known, understood, interpreted, and acted upon through language. Postcolonial theory uses discourse analysis, psychoanalytical approaches, semiotics, and Marxist approaches, but in the end, the purpose is to reveal power relations inherent in any discourse, always in ways that enable subaltern voices to emerge.

Postcolonial theory attempts to go beyond the binaries that shape political and cultural discourse. It suggests that a simple reversal of racial stereotypes, for example, or a naive assertion of nationalism as a response to colonial rule, is not just ineffective, but contains tendencies to reproduce the abuses it resisted in the first place! Instead, postcolonial theory attempts to create what Homi Bhabha has

Gillo Pontecorvo's classic film The Battle of Algiers recounts the Algerian struggle for independence against French colonial forces.

called the "third space" — an approach that highlights the ambiguity, uncertainty, and non-deterministic manner in which struggle and resistance must be carried out. Gayatri Spivak, in a similar vein, has referred to *catachresis*, a form of critique that aims at "reversing, displacing, and seizing the apparatus of value-coding."

This heavy theorizing may all seem like anathema to many activists, and, indeed, postcolonial theory applied to activism may complicate activists' lives in unexpected ways. But, good! In the long-term, activism rooted in postcolonial theory can lead to a far richer engagement with the subaltern — presumably on whose behalf activists do their work. Refusing to already always accept that there is oppression or victimhood can allow subalterns to express their subjectivity — especially on a range of subjects that they are not expected to talk about. For example, a landless peasant or a migrant sweatshop worker producing art, performing poetry, or discussing the meaning of her dreams displaces our notions about how oppressed people behave. The French philosopher Jacques Ranciere, talking about French workers in the mid-19th century, puts it aptly when he says, a worker who sings songs is more dangerous than the worker who shouts slogans. This is because the worker who sings songs has effectively disrupted our notions around how workers are supposed to occupy their symbolic position as workers. Postcolonial theory allows us to see that subaltern people can and do break the symbolic identity that is shackled on to them by activism, opening us to the possibility of pursuing those symbolic transgressions to their revolutionary ends. Thus, postcolonial theory is not just about making activism more effective. Rather, postcolonial theory transforms the very meanings of what constitutes activism itself.

RELATED

Battle of the Camel » p. 14
Hacking Apartheid » p. 38
Welcome to Palestine » p. 90

Civil disobedience » p. 108
Music video » p. 124
Subversive travel » p. 130

Change a name to change the game » p. 142

"Democracy promotion" » p. 180
The Global South » p. 188
The NGO-ization of resistance » p. 200

Power mapping » p. 216
Public narrative (story of self, us, and now) » p. 222

LEARN MORE

Beginning Postcolonialism | John McLeod, Manchester University Press, 2000

Concerning Violence | Göran Olsson, based on Frantz Fanon's essay Concerning Violence, 2014

The Wretched of the Earth | Frantz Fanon, Grove Press, 1963

Can the Subaltern Speak? | Gayatri Spivak, Marxism and the Interpretation of Culture, 1988

○ ○ ○ ○

THE NGO-IZATION OF RESISTANCE

The NGO-ization of politics threatens to turn resistance into a well-mannered, reasonable, salaried, 9-to-5 job. With a few perks thrown in. Real resistance has real consequences. And no salary.

Origins: The term was coined in 2004, though the phenomenon it describes began in the 1980s as one element of the neoliberal project.

"Bel dan pa di zanmi." ("Just because someone is smiling at you doesn't mean they're your friend.")
—Haitian proverb

Arundhati Roy

A hazard facing mass movements is the NGO-ization of resistance. It will be easy to twist what I'm about to say into an indictment of all NGOs. That would be a falsehood. In the murky waters of fake NGOs set up to siphon off grant money or as tax dodges (in states like Bihar, they are given as dowry), of course there are NGOs doing valuable work. But it's important to turn our attention away from the positive work being done by some individual NGOs, and consider the NGO phenomenon in a broader political context.

In India, for instance, the funded NGO boom began in the late 1980s and 1990s. It coincided with the opening of India's markets to neoliberalism *(see: THEORY: Neoliberalism p. 192)*. At the time, the Indian state, in keeping with the requirements

A still from SAIH Norway's satirical video "Who wants to be a volunteer?"

of structural adjustment, was withdrawing funding from rural development, agriculture, energy, transport, and public health. As the state abdicated its traditional role, NGOs moved in to work in these very areas. The difference, of course, is that the funds available to them are a minuscule fraction of the actual cut in public spending. Most large well-funded NGOs are financed and patronized by aid and development agencies, which are in turn funded by Western governments, the World Bank, the UN, and some multinational corporations. Though they may not be the very same agencies, they are certainly part of the same loose, political formation that oversees the neoliberal project and demands the slash in government spending in the first place.

Why should these agencies fund NGOs? Could it be just old-fashioned missionary zeal? Guilt? It's a little more than that.

NGOs give the *impression* that they are filling the vacuum created by a retreating state. And they are, but in a materially inconsequential way. Their *real* contribution is that they defuse political anger and dole out as aid or benevolence what people ought to have by right. They alter the public psyche. They turn people into dependent victims and blunt the edges of political resistance. NGOs form a sort of buffer between the *sarkar* and *public*. Between Empire and its subjects. They have become the arbitrators, the interpreters, the facilitators of the discourse. They play out the role of the "reasonable man" in an unfair, unreasonable war.

In the long run, NGOs are accountable to their funders, not to the people they work among. They're what botanists would call an indicator species. It's almost as though the greater the devastation caused by neoliberalism, the greater the outbreak of NGOs. Nothing illustrates this more poignantly than the phenomenon of the US preparing to invade a country and simultaneously readying NGOs to go in and clean up the devastation.

In order to make sure their funding is not jeopardized and that the governments of the countries they work in will allow them to function, NGOs have to present their work — whether it's in a country devastated by war, poverty, or an epidemic of disease — within a shallow framework more or less shorn of a political or historical context. At any rate, an *inconvenient* historical or political context. It's not for nothing that the "NGO perspective" is becoming increasingly respected.

Apolitical (and therefore, actually, extremely political) distress reports from poor countries and war zones eventually make the (dark) people of those (dark) countries seem like pathological victims. *Another malnourished Indian, another starving Ethiopian, another Afghan refugee camp, another maimed Sudanese . . .* in need of the white man's help *(see: THEORY: Poverty)*. They unwittingly reinforce racist stereotypes and reaffirm the achievements, the comforts, and the compassion (the tough love) of Western civilization, minus the guilt of the history of genocide, colonialism, and slavery. They're the secular missionaries of the modern world.

Eventually — on a smaller scale, but more insidiously — the capital available to NGOs plays the same role in alternative politics as the speculative capital that flows in and out of the economies of poor countries. It begins to dictate the agenda.

It turns confrontation into negotiation. It de-politicizes resistance. It interferes with local peoples' movements that have traditionally been self-reliant. NGOs have funds that can employ local people who might otherwise be activists in resistance movements, but now can feel they are doing some immediate, creative good (and earning a living while they're at it). Charity offers instant gratification to the giver, as well as the receiver, but its side effects can be dangerous. Real political resistance offers no such short cuts.

The NGO-ization of politics threatens to turn resistance into a well-mannered, reasonable, salaried, 9-to-5 job. With a few perks thrown in.

Real resistance has real consequences. And no salary.

Excerpted from Arundhati Roy, The End of Imagination *(Chicago: Haymarket Books, 2016), by permission.*

RELATED

| | | | | | | |

Would you like some structure with your momentum? » *p. 166*

O O O O

"Democracy promotion" » *p. 180*

Neoliberalism » *p. 192*

Postcolonialism » *p. 196*

The Global South » *p. 188*

Pillars of power » *p. 210*

Power mapping » *p. 216*

Spectrum of allies » *p. 232*

LEARN MORE

Public Power in the Age of Empire: Arundhati Roy on War, Resistance, and the Presidency | Democracy Now, 2004

The End of Imagination | Arundhati Roy, Haymarket Books, 2016

The Revolution Will Not Be Funded: Beyond the Non-profit Industrial Complex | Incite! Women of Color Against Violence, South End Press, 2007

METHODOLOGIES

Strategic frameworks and hands-on exercises to help you assess your situation and plan your campaign.

"If you don't know where you're going, you'll end up someplace else."
—Yogi Berra

Tactics are fun, but if you haven't first identified goals and mapped out your strategy for how to achieve them, even the most engaging tactic won't get you closer to where you want to go. That's where these exercises and strategic frameworks come in: They are tools to help you better understand your situation, plan your next steps, assess your progress, and, eventually, win.

ART OF HOSTING

The Art of Hosting is a set of principles and practices for harnessing the self-organizing capacity and collective wisdom of groups to address complex challenges.

Origins: The term "Art of Hosting" was first used (as far as we know) in a workshop hosted by Toke Paludan Møller and others in 1999. Several organizations and networks were a part of its early development, including Days Like This, Engage!, Hara, Interchange, Pioneers of Change, Peer Spirit, The Berkana Institute, World Cafe, and the Shambhala Institute for Authentic Leadership (now ALIA).

"There is no greater power than a community discovering what it cares about."
—Margaret Wheatley

Aerin Dunford and Megan Martin

Based on the assumption that people give their energy and lend their resources to what matters most to them, in work as in life, the Art of Hosting blends a suite of powerful conversational processes to invite people to step in and take charge of the challenges facing them. It can be a powerful tool for activists and organizers

Sergio Beltrán explaining the principles of Open Space, a popular Art of Hosting exercise. Photo: Aerin Dunford | Copyleft

to convene meaningful, empowering, and productive conversations, amongst themselves or in the communities they're seeking to engage.

Groups and organizations using the Art of Hosting as a working practice report better decision making, more efficient and effective capacity building, and greater ability to quickly respond to opportunity, challenge, and change. People who experience the Art of Hosting typically say that they walk away feeling more empowered and able to help guide meetings and conversations towards more effective and desirable outcomes.

In our work as creative activists, we've all participated in a meeting that feels like a waste of time, conversations that feel more like debates, and invitations to provide input that turn out to be something altogether different. People want to contribute, but they can't see how. Some voices dominate, while others are barely heard. Or, we have a great conversation, but then struggle to summarize the key points or priority tasks arising from it. As leaders, we want the best contributions of everyone *(see: PRINCIPLE: We are all leaders)*, but often don't know how to get them. The Art of Hosting offers groups a number of collaborative methods that work well together — including Circle, World Cafe, Appreciative Inquiry, Open Space Technology, ProAction Cafe, storytelling and more — to address issues like these.

The Art of Hosting is being used by a variety of groups — families, organizations, governments — and in many sectors, including healthcare, education, human rights, youth, and justice, to name a few. It has been used to convene a collective and simultaneous conversation of over 10,000 people in cities across Israel/historic Palestine to talk about social justice; as a transformative container for wide collaboration within the European Commission and other EU institutions; for rethinking large and complex citywide systems in Columbus, Ohio, US; and it serves as the underlying *modus operandi* at the permaculture demonstration village, Kufunda, in Ruwa, Zimbabwe.

As a practice, the Art of Hosting offers those who feel called to grapple with large issues both a framework and a practice that hones their skills, builds their capacity, and invites the participation of all. Because it can be used in conjunction with many other methodologies or practices, it can be thought of as a sort of "operating system" that focuses the group on effective and grounded communication.

POTENTIAL RISKS

The Art of Hosting is a practice that involves both a set of specific exercises and an overarching commitment to trust in the capacity, intelligence, and potential of a given group of people. It's not a series of steps to be followed, but rather a muscle that requires constant exercise. Forgetting to have patience with the practice (and with yourself) can be an obstacle. It's also important that leaders or power brokers are truly open to the input or results of these participatory processes. If there are hidden agendas or predetermined outcomes, participants will often find themselves disillusioned or disempowered by the process.

HOW TO USE

For a more in-depth introduction to Art of Hosting, check out the Art of Hosting website. The best way to start using the Art of Hosting is to find other practitioners and try out the processes together. We suggest looking out for opportunities to learn alongside other practitioners (whether a training opportunity, or a chance to participate in an Art of Hosting process near you), and then putting that muscle to work in your communities and groups.

RELATED

Al faza'a (a surge of solidarity) » p. 172

LEARN MORE

Art of Hosting

Art of Hosting Mexico | Facebook

Art of Hosting Online Community

PILLARS OF POWER

Use a *pillars of power* analysis to identify the institutions without whose support your target would collapse, and to strategize ways to weaken or remove those institutional "pillars."

Origins: Gandhi, Gene Sharp, Robert Helvey.

"First they ignore you, then they ridicule you, then they fight you, and then you win."
—Gandhi

Eric Stoner

Many believe that "power grows out of the barrel of a gun," as Mao Zedong famously said. However, research and experience show that power stems not just from a powerful opponent's ability to use force, but also from the consent and cooperation of the institutions and organizations that sustain the oppressor: the media, the army, the police, the courts, the universities, organized labor, international backers, and others.

Use a *pillars of power* analysis to identify the institutions without whose support your target would collapse, and to strategize ways to weaken or remove those institutional "pillars," so that the foundation that sustains the target begins to crumble and the system falls. Once you understand the various institutions that enable a specific oppressive regime or status quo situation to maintain its power, you can investigate how to neutralize, undermine, or withdraw the foundations that the oppressive system depends on, and reduce its power.

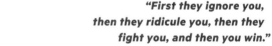

Some of these pillars, such as the military, the police, and the courts, are coercive in nature, compelling obedience through force or the threat of force, while other pillars, like the media, the education system, and religious institutions, support the system through their influence over culture and popular opinion. Hence, the power of even the most charismatic or ruthless leader is contingent upon the support of key institutions, themselves vulnerable to popular action or withdrawal of consent from the general population.

In February 2011, Egyptian President Mubarak was forced to leave office when several of his key institutional pillars cracked — the army and business community foremost among them — removing their support for him. (Unfortunately, in the long run, the Egyptian revolution was unable to assemble a strong enough foundation of its own to counter the regime's largest pillar, the military, which retook control in a coup in 2013.).

As another example, a major turning point leading to the downfall of Serbian President Slobodan Milošević in 2000 was when the police refused to enforce his orders to fire on protesters. This was the result of a deliberate strategy by the leading opposition group Otpor to reach out to the police and remind them that their families and friends were among the demonstrators. Desertions, especially from high-level military positions, are a clear sign that this crucial pillar of support has begun to crumble.

Power ultimately rests not in the grip of presidents, generals, and billionaires, but in the hands of millions of ordinary people who keep society running smoothly on a day-to-day basis, and who can shut it down should they so choose. This is the meaning of the slogan "people power." One of the main reasons that so many injustices persist is not that the powerful can simply do whatever they want with impunity, but that most people are ignorant of the power they can wield by withdrawing their consent *(see: TACTIC: General strike).*

Samson destroying the temple of the Philistines by pulling down the supporting pillars.

This understanding of power has been repeatedly vindicated in recent decades, as numerous dictators and extremely repressive regimes have been toppled by unarmed people with minimal violence but much courage and creativity. These successful nonviolent struggles simply cannot be explained by someone who sees violence as the only, or even the primary, mechanism of power.

Spheres of Influence/Power Map

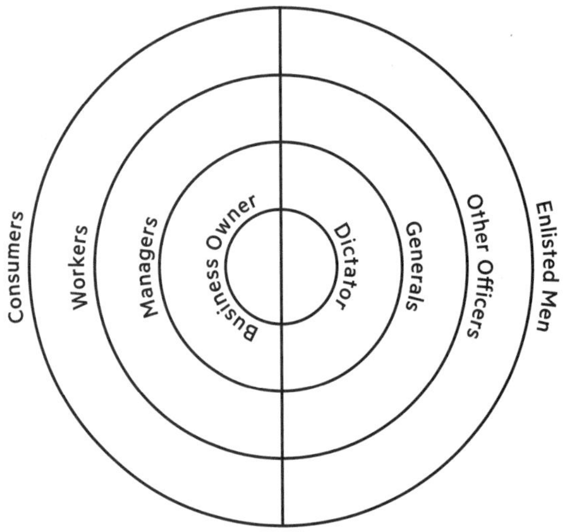

POTENTIAL RISKS

This tool is great for starting out with people-power strategic planning, and will develop a big picture overview of the vulnerability and strengths of the system you are fighting. But don't mistake this for a detailed road map for your campaign — follow up this tool with others mentioned in the "How To Use" section. And, as in real life, if you end up pushing the pillars of support in towards the center rather than pulling them away, the roof will not come down. Take this into account when determining which pillars you will target, and how.

RELATED

Battle of the Camel » p. 14
Schools of Struggle » p. 60
Stolen Gas Campaign » p. 72
Stop Prawer Plan » p. 78

Civil disobedience » p. 108
Divestment » p. 112
Jail solidarity » p. 118

Activate international mechanisms » p. 138
Would you like some structure with your momentum? » p. 166

Al faza'a (a surge of solidarity) » p. 172
Baltajiah (thugs) » p. 176
Neoliberalism » p. 192
The NGO-ization of resistance » p. 200

Power mapping » p. 216
SMART objectives » p. 226
Spectrum of allies » p. 232

HOW TO USE

1 Draw a building, represented by a roof that is a simple triangle, with pillars holding it up. Label the roof with the name of the system, regime, or issue you are working on.

2 Identify the "pillars" that constitute the institutions that support the target (educational institutions, the media, the military, corporations, etc.). Start generally, but refine and specify as much as you can about each pillar. For example, if you identify the police or the military as a major pillar generally, then sub-labelling them more specifically "Capitol District Police" or "President's Special Forces" will give you a more precise picture of the issue and a better framework for strategic planning.

3 Take a moment to identify which pillars are most critical to holding up the system. Perhaps some pillars are bigger than others in your drawing, representing the relative strength of one institution in supporting the system to another lesser institution. Then, compare and identify your ability to impact or reach whomever makes up the pillars that are both critical to the system and vulnerable to your impact. These are the places where your campaign has great potential.

Pillars of Power

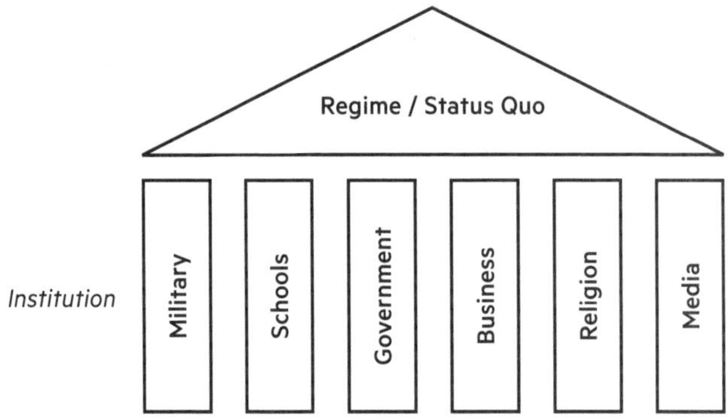

4 One way to determine where you may have the most potential to impact the strength of a pillar is by analyzing the internal construction of each pillar. Start by drawing a circle that represents a cross section of the pillar, with concentric circles that you can label with the individuals or groups that compose the pillar itself. Be specific about elements of the support structures,

with the center being the most impacted or powerful (the dictator or general might be in the center of the military pillar, with other leadership in the next circle, then regular troops, then veterans, military families, etc.). As you move out from the center, the power the groups or individuals hold changes, and their connection or loyalty to the institution often diminishes. This will help you visually assess where you could have the most impact on a pillar, and which constituencies you may be able to reach as you try to break down support for the system.

5 Now, use this big picture analysis with a more in-depth strategic planning tool such as spectrum of allies, which identifies the relative resource cost of moving specific constituencies *(see: METHODOLOGY: Spectrum of allies p. 232)*; SWOT matrix, which correlates internal and external plans *(see: METHODOLOGY: SWOT matrix)*; or points of intervention, which hones tactical plans *(see: METHODOLOGY: Points of intervention)*. There is often a benefit of using more than one tool at a time, helping to identify missing pieces and bringing in a specificity that will help to create a more effective strategic plan.

LEARN MORE

This is an Uprising: How Nonviolent Revolt is Shaping the 21st Century | ThisIsAnUprising.org, 2016

People Power | Lisa Fithian, 2013

On Strategic Nonviolent Conflict: Thinking about the Fundamentals | Robert Helvey, Albert Einstein Institution, 2004

Waging Nonviolent Struggle: Twentieth-Century Practice and Twenty-First-Century Potential | Gene Sharp, Porter Sargent, 2005

CANVAS Manual | Center for Applied Nonviolent Action and Strategies, 2004

A Force More Powerful | International Center on Nonviolent Conflict, 2000

POWER MAPPING

Before you "fight the power," make sure you know who *has* the power. Power mapping can help you identify who your campaign should be targeting and how to get to them.

Origins: It is difficult to pinpoint the exact origins of power mapping, but the tool has been used widely in advocacy and campaigning since the 1980s.

"The most common way people give up their power is by thinking they don't have any."
—Alice Walker

Andrew Boyd

To win a campaign, you need to correctly identify who has the power to fix the problem you want fixed. Then you need to pressure them to make the right decision. Power mapping is a tool to not only identify who holds that power, but, crucially, who holds influence over that person, and, therefore, who to target with your direct actions and campaign activities *(see: PRINCIPLE: Choose your target wisely)*. A power map, properly done, can reveal these relationships and power dynamics and help you design a winning strategy for your campaign.

Let's say a Canadian mining company is trying to extract minerals from the land surrounding your community in Mali. As a result, the land is getting polluted, seriously affecting your family's and neighbors' health. Who do you target? The company? And if so, do you target the regional director in Mali or the international

CEO in Canada? Who ultimately has the power to close the mine? And what kind of power can you leverage to make them do it? Doing a power map of the whole situation can help you answer these questions. It might tell you that you shouldn't, in fact, target the company because you won't be able to build enough direct leverage over them. Instead, the power map might indicate you should target the Malian government — to pass a law, or insist on a clean-up. But who exactly? Everyone from the local mayor up to the President has some degree of power in the situation, as well as varying degrees of influence over each other. A power map can help illuminate these relationships and suggest the best way forward.

It's critically important to do a power map *before* you start campaigning. Going after the wrong targets can be damaging to your motivation and resources. It is important to make sure that you're on the right track before you start!

You may find, as the farmworkers who organized the Taco Bell Boycott did, that even after correctly identifying your target, and campaigning against them for a while, you can't mobilize enough power to directly pressure them to fix the problem *(see: STORY: Taco Bell Boycott)*. That's when you need to focus your energies on pressuring what are called "secondary targets" — power-holders who can influence your primary target. If they feel enough pressure from you, they'll lean on the primary target to give into your demands. Power mapping helps you draw all the lines of influence between your primary target and all the other stakeholders involved — including you.

Protesters occupy the roof of the National Congress of Brazil in Brasília on June 17, 2013. Photo: Marcello Casal Jr./ABr | CC BY 3.0

POTENTIAL RISKS

People come and go, and the power landscape constantly shifts, so you will need to periodically revisit and revise your power map to maintain a current and accurate picture of the power dynamics your campaign must navigate. Also, structures of power not only vary across time, but can also vary from place to place — so don't assume that the same problem will have the same power map in two different geographical areas. You need to spend the time to make sure your map is detailed and accurate.

HOW TO USE

1. Identify the problem you are trying to fix. Expand your knowledge until you have a broad understanding of the issue and the forces involved.
2. Identify the main stakeholders. These stakeholders generally include:
   - those responsible for creating the problem;
   - those who have the power to fix the problem but are not doing so;
   - those who are geographically relevant to the issue;
   - those who are working to fix the problem;
   - and don't forget to include you and your group, too.

   You'll end up with a long list of institutions (both formal and informal), organizations, influential people, media, and assorted individuals that are relevant to your issue. Keep this list handy!
3. Research the stakeholders. There are some institutions on your list, but institutions don't make decisions, people do. So, you've got to find out who makes the decisions in those institutions. And then you've got to try to answer a few questions about these people: Do they agree or disagree with you on this issue? How much power do they have over this issue?
4. Plot where all the stakeholders stand. Draw out a version of the "Power Mapping: Axes" diagram on a board or big chart paper. Put each stakeholder on its own post-it. Then, depending on how supportive they are, and how much power they have over the issue, you can place them on the board.

Power Mapping: Axes

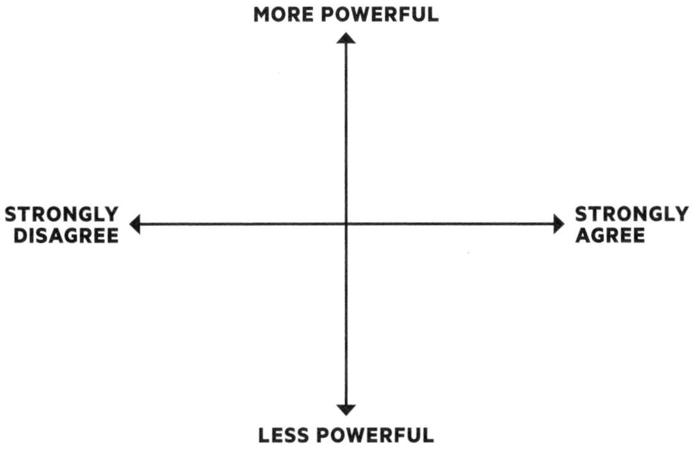

5 Identify your primary target. This is the point when you figure out who has the most influence over the issue and who is most likely to give you what you want. The perfect target (and perfection rarely exists in real life) would be both very powerful and already supportive (or at least easily accessible and open to supporting you). The hardest target to move, but the kind you will often face, and be forced to take on, is someone with a lot of power who strongly disagrees with you. (If you can't decide on a single primary target, but only have the capacity to focus on one, proceed to the next step with your most likely candidates. The next step looks at your proximity or potential to reach each target, and may help you choose which one is best to focus on.)

6 Map the power relationships around your primary target. Take the post-it of the stakeholder you've identified as your primary target and place it in the middle of another big sheet of paper. Are they influenced by any of the other names you have written down on the post-its? Who can sway them? Arrange the other stakeholder post-its on the big paper in relationship to the key target. Draw circles and arrows of relationship similar to "Power Mapping: Relationships." Make sure to include yourself and your potential relationship to all stakeholders in this diagram whenever possible.

continued on next page ›

7 Map the power relationships around your secondary targets. You may not be able to move your primary target directly. The only way to get to them is through other stakeholders you've identified in Step 6 who have some influence on them. These are your secondary targets. But who are *they* influenced by? To find out, make a separate power map for each of these stakeholders. Power mapping can be meticulous work! Again, include yourself and your potential relationship to anyone on this diagram so it is clear how to proceed with campaign planning.

8 Use this analysis to plan your campaign. Now, make sure to actually use this research and analysis to create a plan that targets those who can actually give you what you want, rather than just the people you can reach easily.

9 Revisit and revise. At key campaign junctures, and as power shifts or you learn more about who holds it, revisit and revise these maps as needed. You'll know when!

Power Mapping: Relationships

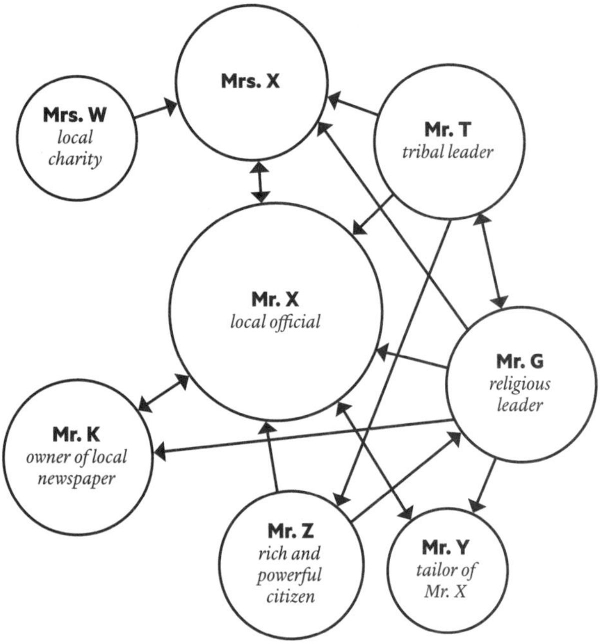

RELATED

Schools of Struggle » p. 60
Sign Language Sit-In » p. 66
Stop Prawer Plan » p. 78

Divestment » p. 112

Postcolonialism » p. 196
The NGO-ization of resistance » p. 200

Pillars of power » p. 210
SMART objectives » p. 226
Spectrum of allies » p. 232
The onion tool » p. 238

LEARN MORE

A Guide to Power Mapping | Move to Amend

Just and Democratic Governance: Power | International Governance Team, ActionAid, 2012

PUBLIC NARRATIVE (STORY OF SELF, US, AND NOW)

A leadership practice that uses an interrelated set of stories — stories of self, us, and now — to understand our sources of motivation, build community identity around shared values, and move people to action.

Origins: Marshall Ganz, a long-time organizer in the migrant farmworkers movement in the US, and currently a Senior Lecturer at Kennedy School of Government at Harvard, developed the public narrative methodology in the 1990s as part of a values-based community organizing framework.

"If I am not for myself, who will be? And if I am for myself alone, what am 'I'? And if not now, when?"
—Rabbi Hillel the Elder

Nisreen Haj Ahmad

A good story has the power to change the world. The *public narrative* methodology trains organizers, activists, and community leaders to share their personal stories more effectively, in order to build a sense of community around shared values and experiences, and ultimately to move large numbers of people to action on an issue or cause.

Public narrative is useful when you are forming a new team or expanding a group to bring them together around values and choices. It is also used when you are preparing your community or team to deal with a challenge, whether internal or external to the organization. The most obvious use of narrative is to move people to action; the less obvious use is to decide strategy. Often, hidden in people's stories of what choices they made, and what calls them to leadership, is the answer to what our strategy should be *(see: METHODOLOGY: Narrative power analysis)*. Public narrative is also used to awaken people to injustice, and to their own agency in confronting it, especially within communities or groups that have been oppressed for centuries.

Public narrative is made up of three interwoven stories, that, once honed, the storyteller should be able to tell in a total of under five minutes:

- First is *the story of self:* I tell my personal story so that you understand what calls me to leadership on this cause. What challenges have I faced and what choices have I made that show why I am moved to leadership on this cause? In my story, I describe the results of my choices and shed light on what gives me hope.
- Second is *the story of us:* I seek to learn the stories of members of my community and I weave them together around the values that we share. This story describes who we are, what our shared challenges are, and some milestones in the journey we've walked so far.
- Third is *the story of now:* What is the price of inaction? I share images portraying the consequences of inaction and other images showing what our action can achieve. After creating a sense of urgency and hope, I end my narrative with a specific and doable call to action.

Public narrative is a practice of leadership; it's the *why* of organizing — the art of translating values into action through stories.

Marshall Ganz, developer of the public narrative methodology. Photo: flyoverthis | CC BY-SA 2.0

POTENTIAL RISKS

Watch out for the following mistakes when you develop your public narrative:

- Your *story of self* should include not just the challenges you faced, but the choices you made. The goal is to motivate action and emphasize agency. If you don't include the choices you made and the outcomes of these choices, then it may sound like a victim's story.
- Often people end with a very general call to action such as "join our movement" or "adopt our cause." The best calls to action are the most specific. For example, "Join our movement; join the march on May 5th at 2 p.m. from the central station towards Parliament to submit the petition with 20,000 voices."
- If you're telling a *story of self* and a *story of now* without a *story of us,* you're basically playing the hero and asking people to follow you, instead of engaging in collective action and encouraging them to develop their own leadership.
- This is not a public speaking exercise; it is an exercise to develop agency and build community. It's not to put *gloss* on a speech but to bring out the *glow* from within us that moves us for our cause.

Remember, having a strong public narrative capable of mobilizing people does not replace the need for a strong campaign strategy and program of action, both online and in the field. Similarly, a good *story of us* that ties a group together around shared values and experiences does not replace the need to establish shared norms and culture around leadership, decision making, commitment, and accountability, among other things.

HOW TO USE

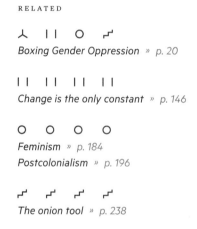

A skill session that trains leaders in public narrative would generally proceed in three steps.

1 Show examples of good narrative.

2 Explain the elements of each of the three stories — self, us, and now.

3 Have the participants develop their own narrative and coach each other's stories.

For a big group, a full-day session would be appropriate; for a small group and a good trainer, a few-hours-long session would suffice.

For a more in-depth introduction to public narrative and how to use it in practice, check out Marshall Ganz's foundational text, *Public Narrative, Collective Action, and Power.*

RELATED

Boxing Gender Oppression » p. 20

Change is the only constant » p. 146

Feminism » p. 184
Postcolonialism » p. 196

The onion tool » p. 238

LEARN MORE

Public Narrative: Self, Us, and Now | Marshall Ganz, 2011

Public Narrative, Collective Action, and Power | Marshall Ganz, in *Accountability Through Public Opinion: From Inertia to Public Action*, 2011

SMART OBJECTIVES

SMART is a tool to set short- and medium-term objectives. It helps us be more precise, realistic, and effective across the duration of a campaign, as well as assess whether we successfully met our objectives.

Origins: This methodology originated in the world of marketing and business management, and was appropriated by activists to help them plan campaigns.

"What can we do today, so that tomorrow we can do what we are unable to do today?"
—Paulo Freire

Marcelo Marquesini

Elaborating a campaign objective might appear to be a simple task, however, it is quite common in the activist world to find poorly formulated objectives that are impossible to reach. This kind of error can have a major negative impact on the success of a campaign.

The SMART tool is a way to plan short- and medium-term objectives that are Specific, Measurable, Achievable, Realistic, and Time-bound, and that increase the likelihood of a campaign's success. It's a tool that helps people involved in a campaign or action maintain their focus and align their expectations.

Direct action with 350 crosses by the Basta de Mortes no Trânsito (Enough Traffic Killings) campaign in Recife, Brazil, 2016. Photo: Ju Brainer

The formulation of a SMART objective begins by determining a *problem*, a *desired change*, and a *vision for the future*, which then serve as the basis for additional analyzes, including: context analysis, an analysis of the strengths, weaknesses, opportunities, and threats *(see: METHODOLOGY: SWOT matrix)*, and a mapping of the actors that can support or hinder your goals *(see: METHODOLOGY: Power mapping p. 216)*.

The results of all these analyzes will orient the process of defining a SMART objective.

POTENTIAL RISKS

Not all SMART objectives will strictly follow the five criteria. Be careful with the different interpretations given to each of the tool's initials and don't let your objective lose its SMART connotation. In many occasions, the letter A can be switched for Attainable, Assignable, Action-oriented, or Actionable, and the letter R for Reasonable, Relevant, Resourced, or Results-based. The SMART methodology is more suited for short- and medium-term objectives. The definition of what is short- and medium-term will depend on your campaign and the larger context in which it is happening. For some campaigns, short can mean a few weeks, while for others it can mean two or even three years.

HOW TO USE

Specific - An objective must be simple and well-defined, communicating what you wish to happen and avoiding dubious interpretations. This can best be achieved by using strong action verbs, such as: expose, develop, build, plan, execute, perform. Some questions that can make your objective more specific are:

- What exactly are we hoping to achieve?
- Why is this important?
- What are the benefits to reaching this goal?
- How evident is the result?

Measurable - When an objective is measurable, we can monitor our actions as we progress. The possibility of measuring allows comparisons. If you can't measure, you won't be able to manage your actions and evaluate your results. Some of the questions that can help with this are:

- How will we know that the change has happened?
- What are the indicators of success?
- What benefits are created, what targets are hit, what values are increased or decreased, what places/people/objects/fauna/flora are protected, what territories/rights are guaranteed?
- Can these measurements be obtained?

continued on next page ›

Achievable - In social change efforts, objectives can be bold and challenging, but they should never be impossible to achieve — and if the SMART logic is employed correctly, they won't be. If the objective requires resources that your group simply doesn't have, then everyone will be frustrated. Consider the following questions:

- Has anyone ever done this successfully?
- Is this possible in the deadline we have set?
- Are all the restrictions evident? (e.g. logistic, legal, cultural)

Realistic - Can often be mistaken for Achievable. The basic difference is that in many cases while the objective can be achieved, it is not particularly realistic for the people involved due to some form of conflict. In certain cases, an internal change in the pattern of collective organization will be necessary to turn the objective into a realistic one. You should consider these factors:

- Is your group willing to fight for this objective?
- Is this objective aligned with your group's mission and vision?
- Are any ethical principles jeopardized by this objective?
- Are there enough resources available?

Time-bound - A time limit means setting a deadline to reach the objective. This criteria can slightly overlap with Specific. Time-bound provides the necessary impetus to keep people motivated to make things happen, and the start and end periods must be achievable and realistic. This time period must not be so short that the objective is impossible to reach, nor so long that the group disintegrates over time. Deadlines create the necessary urgency and stimulate action. Try using questions such as:

- Is there a window of opportunity within which we need to act? (e.g. before the next election, board meeting, etc.)
- When will this objective be reached?

RELATED

Schools of Struggle » *p. 60*
Sign Language Sit-In » *p. 66*

Civil disobedience » *p. 108*

Pillars of power » *p. 210*
Power mapping » *p. 216*
Spectrum of allies » *p. 232*

LEARN MORE

Objectives | The Change Agency, Australia

Why Campaigns, Not Protests, Get the Goods | George Lakey, Waging Nonviolence, 2016

SPECTRUM OF ALLIES

Use a spectrum-of-allies analysis to identify the social groups that are affected by your issue, and then focus your action or campaign on shifting one or more of those groups closer to your position.

Origins: George Lakey, Training for Change.

"In the end we will remember not the words of our enemies, but the silence of our friends."
—Martin Luther King, Jr.

Nadine Bloch

Movements seldom win by overpowering the opposition; they win by shifting support out from under it. Use a spectrum-of-allies analysis to identify the social groups (students, workers) that are affected by your issue, and locate those groups along a spectrum, from *active opposition* to *active allies*, so you can focus your efforts on shifting those groups closer to your position. Identifying specific stakeholders (e.g. not just students, but students at public colleges; not just workers, but domestic workers) can help you identify the most effective ways of moving different social groups closer to your position, in order to win your campaign.

When mapping out your campaign, it is useful to look at society as a collection of specific communities, blocs, or networks, some of which are institutions (unions, churches, schools), others of which are less visible or cohesive, like youth subcultures or demographic groupings. The more precisely you can identify stakeholders and impacted communities, the better you can prepare to persuade those groups or individuals to move closer to your position. You can then weigh the relative costs and benefits of focusing on different blocs.

Evaluating your spectrum of allies can help you avoid some common pitfalls. Some activist groups, for instance, only concern themselves with their active allies, which runs the risk of "preaching to the choir" — building marginal subcultures that are incomprehensible to everyone else, while ignoring the people you actually need to convince. Others behave as if everyone who disagrees with their position is an active opponent, playing out the "story of the righteous few," acting as if the whole world is against them. Yet others take a "speak truth to power" approach, figuring that through moral appeal or force of logical argument, they can somehow win over their most entrenched active opponents. All three of these extreme approaches virtually guarantee failure. Movements and campaigns are won not by overpowering one's active opposition, but by shifting each group one notch around the spectrum (passive allies into active allies, neutrals into passive allies, and passive opponents into neutrals), thereby increasing people power in favor of change and weakening your opposition.

For example, in 1964 in the US, the Student Nonviolent Coordinating Committee (SNCC), a major driver of the African-American civil rights movement in the racially segregated South, realized that in order to win desegregation and voting rights

The radicalization of white students from the North who bussed down to the South for the Freedom Summer campaign helped trigger a critical shift in public opinion in favor of civil rights in America in the 1960s. Photo: Ted Polumbaum/ Newseum

for African Americans, they needed to make active allies of sympathetic white northerners. Many students in the North were sympathetic, but had no entry point into the movement. They didn't need to be educated or convinced, they needed an invitation to enter the struggle. (Or in the spectrum-of-allies schema, they needed to be moved from passive allies into active allies.) Moreover, these white students had extended communities of white families and friends who were not directly impacted by the struggles of African-American southerners. As the struggle escalated, these groups could be shifted from neutral to passive allies or even active allies.

Based on this analysis, the SNCC made a strategic decision to focus on reaching neutral white communities in the North by engaging sympathetic white students in their Freedom Summer program. Busloads of students traveled to the South to assist with voter registration, and many were deeply radicalized in the process. They witnessed lynchings, violent police abuse, and angry white mobs, all a response to black Southerners simply trying to exercise their right to vote.

Many wrote letters home to their parents, who suddenly had a personal connection to the struggle. This triggered another desired shift: Their families became passive allies, often bringing their workplaces and social networks with them. The students, meanwhile, returned to school in the fall as active allies, and proceeded to organize their campuses — more shifts in the direction of civil rights. The result: a profound transformation of the political landscape.

This cascading shift of support wasn't spontaneous; it was part of a deliberate movement strategy that, to this day, carries profound lessons for other movements.

POTENTIAL RISKS

Watch out for very broad or generic identification of the blocs/groups in the pie chart. Without enough precision this tool won't help you identify specific communication tactics for reaching particular groups. Nor will you be able to get an accurate read on the true resource costs of reaching those groups.

Spectrum of Allies

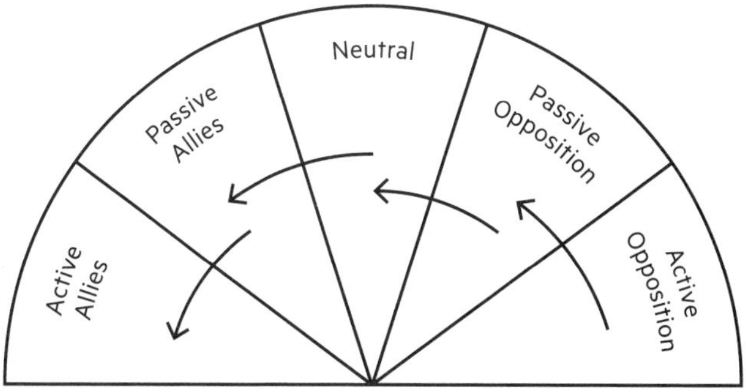

HOW TO USE

Use this tool to identify the constituencies that could be moved one notch along the spectrum, as well as to assess the relative costs of reaching, educating, or mobilizing each of these constituencies. Do not use this tool to identify your arch enemies and go after them — it's the people in the middle you'll most often want to focus on. The groupings or individuals you identify should be as specific as possible: not just unions, for instance, but specific unions. The more specific you can be, the better this tool will serve you.

Here's how to do a spectrum-of-allies analysis:

1. Set up a "half-pie" drawing (see diagram). Label the entire drawing with the name of the specific movement or campaign you are discussing, and put yourself on the left side, with your opposition on the right side.
2. Divide the half-pie into five slices:
   - *active allies*, or people who agree with you and are fighting alongside you;
   - *passive allies*, or people who agree with you but aren't (yet) doing anything about it;
   - *neutrals*, or the unengaged and uninformed;
   - *passive opposition*, or people who disagree with you but aren't actively trying to stop you; and
   - *active opposition*, or people who not only disagree with you, but are actively organizing against you.

   In the appropriate wedges, place different constituencies, organizations, or individuals. Spend a significant amount of time brainstorming the groups and individuals that belong in each of the sections. Be specific: list them with as

continued on next page ›

many identifying characteristics as possible. And make sure to cover every wedge; neglecting sections will limit your strategic planning and your potential effectiveness.

3 Step back and see if you're being specific enough. For every group or bloc you listed in the diagram, ask yourself whether you could be more specific — are there more adjectives or qualifiers you could add to give more definition to the description? You might be tempted to say "mothers," but the reality might be that "wealthy mothers who live in gated communities" might belong in one wedge, and "mothers who work as market vendors" would belong in another. The more specific you can be, the better this tool will serve you.

4 When you come up against the limits of your knowledge, make sure to start a list of follow-up questions — and commit to doing the research you'll need to get the answers.

The spectrum of allies can also work well in combination with other methodologies:

- First, use pillars of power to map out the biggest forces at play.
- Combine with a SWOT matrix in order to help you identify all key constituencies.
- Follow up with points of intervention in order to identify tactics and actions to engage the key constituencies you've identified.

RELATED

Battle of the Camel » p. 14
Burmese Students' Long March » p. 26
Flower Speech Campaign » p. 32
Honk at Parliament » p. 44
Stop Prawer Plan » p. 78
Welcome to Palestine » p. 90
Zapatista Caravan » p. 100

Divestment » p. 112
Music video » p. 124
Subversive travel » p. 130
Activate international mechanisms » p.138

Would you like some structure with your momentum? » p. 166

Al faza'a (a surge of solidarity) » p. 172

Pillars of power » p. 210
Power mapping » p. 216

LEARN MORE

Spectrum of Allies | War Resisters' International

Exercises: Identifying Allies and Opponents | New Tactics in Human Rights

Moving Your Allies: A Follow-Up Exercise | Training for Change

Know Your Allies, Your Opponents, and Everyone In-Between | George Lakey, Waging Nonviolence, 2012

Civil Resistance and the 3.5% Rule | Erika Chenoweth, Rational Insurgent / TEDxBoulder, 2013

THE ONION TOOL

People in power aren't as simple as we think. What they say they want is rarely what they really want, never mind what they can't live without. The onion tool peels back the rhetoric to give a deeper picture.

Origins: The onion tool was first developed by Ian Mitroff and Thierry Pauchant in the 1990s as a means of managing crises and conflicts, but its use has expanded to many different fields.

"We are what we pretend to be, so we must be careful about what we pretend to be."
—*Kurt Vonnegut Jr.*

Nils Amar Tegmo

People — including politicians and other people with power — aren't as one-dimensional as we might think. What they say isn't always what they actually want or need. Rather, they have complex layers of needs, interests, and positions; some may be visible and others invisible. The onion tool helps us peel back their political rhetoric to build a deeper, more complex understanding of what motivates particular individuals in power, so we can better work with (or against) them.

The onion tool makes a critical distinction between a powerful person's positions, interests, and needs.

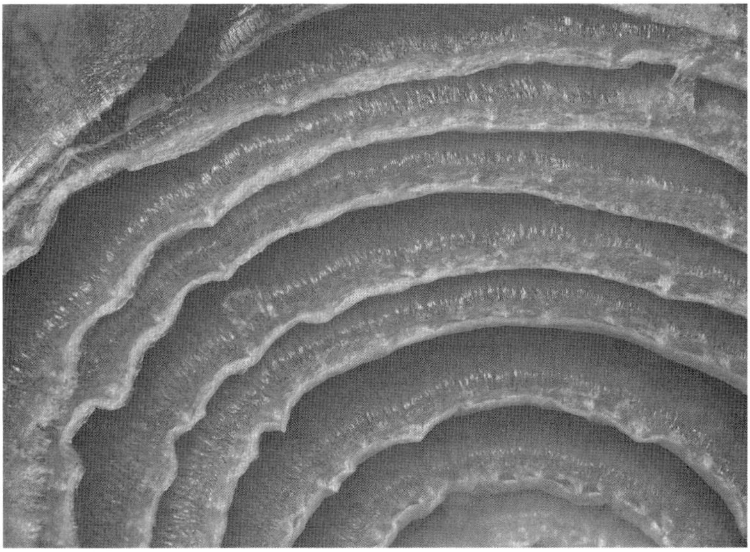

The onion tool can peel back layers to expose desires and needs at the core.
Photo: theilr | CC BY-SA 2.0

A **position** is *what we say we want.* But talk can be cheap, especially from powerful politicians and the business elite. If we assume they're telling us the full truth, we will never get the broader picture. This does not mean we need to be generally distrustful, only that it is advisable to think clearly, rationally, and critically when listening to what the powerful say.

An **interest**, on the other hand, is *what we really want.* Our interests are not always evident from our stated position. For example, the interest of a politician may be to consolidate power and increase wealth. The interest of Coca-Cola or Shell is most likely to accumulate financial gain at the expense of others. Meanwhile they're talking about the good of the nation, and promising happiness to anyone who drinks Coca-Cola. There is a clear difference between what they say they want and what they really want.

At the heart of it all are our **needs.** This is *what we must have* and is often non-negotiable. For an individual it may be our values, commitments, beliefs, or ethics. It is the innermost layer and generally where we are most honest. It is, of course, deep inside and often hidden, so understanding the inner workings of other people is not always easy.

So what does all this have to do with activism and campaigning? Well, if we're going to be strategic about changing society for the better, we need to assess and analyze the positions, interests, and needs of those with power. By understanding powerful individuals at a more profound level, we can choose our targets wisely, communicate with them more strategically (and when needed, diplomatically), and better identify conflicts of interests and potential alliances.

Also, while positions are generally public, true interests are not. Sometimes exposing your opponent's true interest can undermine their credibility, and move your cause closer to victory.

The ability to distinguish between what people say they want, what they really want, and what they can't live without has many practical applications. For example, the onion tool is great for conflict management within teams of activists or campaigners when disagreements arise. It can help you identify what really matters to you and your colleagues and help you determine shared priorities.

The Onion Tool

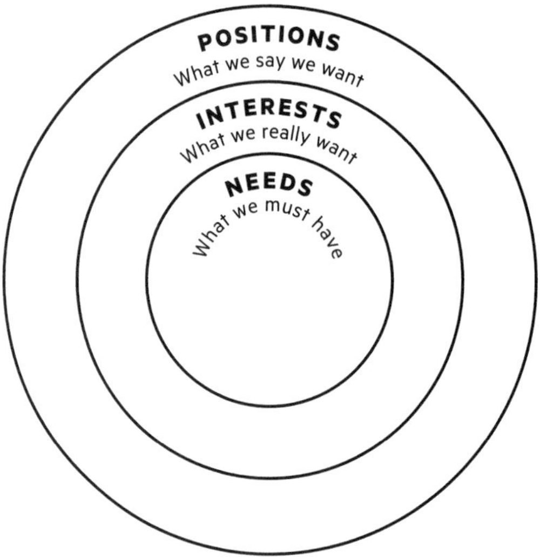

POTENTIAL RISKS

Determining a person's needs can be more difficult than determining their positions or interests because their needs often remain unspoken and are generally less obvious and more idiosyncratic.

HOW TO USE

1. Draw three concentric circles.
2. In the outermost circle write "Positions," in the middle circle write "Interests," and in the innermost circle write "Needs."
3. Select an individual to base the onion tool on. This will likely be the name of an individual stakeholder who is relevant to your work.
4. Identify their positions. What are they saying publicly? What do they say they want?
5. Identify their interests. Can you deduce their actual interests? What do they really want?
6. Identify their needs. What is it that they can't live without? To what or whom is their innermost commitment?
7. You now have a better understanding of where the individual in question stands. Repeating the process for various stakeholders will help you ascertain whom to target and with whom you may be able to forge an alliance.
8. As your campaign evolves, you can use this tool neatly in tandem with the power mapping methodology, using the latter to identify key stakeholders, and the former to peel back each stakeholder's layers of interests *(see: METHODOLOGY: Power mapping p. 216).*

RELATED

Schools of Struggle » *p. 60*

Change is the only constant » *p. 146*

Power mapping » *p. 216*
Public narrative (story of self, us, and now) » *p. 222*

LEARN MORE

Positions, Interests, and Needs | The Network University

Just and Democratic Governance: Power | International Governance Team, ActionAid, 2012

CONTRIBUTORS

Juman Abujbara is a social change campaigner, human rights defender, and aspiring philosopher based in Amman, Jordan.

Nisreen Haj Ahmad is a Palestinian activist, organizer, and co-founder of Ahel.org. She trains and coaches people and organizations to run campaigns in the Middle East, using Marshall Ganz' organizing framework.

Safa' Al Jayoussi is a leading environmentalist and an activist in the field of climate and energy campaigns in the Arab world. She has launched and implemented campaigns including an anti-nuclear operation in Jordan and a major push during and prior to COP21 to advocate and mobilize for a new climate agreement signed by Arab leaders.

Ribal Al-Kurdi is a theater actor and dance trainer, has a law degree from Al-Quds University, and is the Executive Director of the Alrowwad Cultural and Arts Society in Bethlehem, Palestine.

D. 'Alwan is an Iraqi-American born in the United States who has lived, worked, traveled, and studied in the Middle East and North Africa. Her work has included making guerilla public art and culture jamming, documentary video, violence prevention education, facilitating art programs in US prisons, and designing affordable housing.

Loay Bakr, a graduate of the Faculty of Law at Helwan University, has been an activist in Egyptian civil society since 2008 and has participated in the observation of municipal and parliamentary elections. He was part of the 2011 Egyptian revolution and is co-founder of the El-Dostour Party, member of the coalition *Gabhet Tarik El Thawra*, and co-founder of Boycott, Divestment, Sanctions (BDS) Egypt.

Hoda Baraka is an Egyptian environmentalist currently working as Global Communications Manager for 350.org, which is an international campaign working to build a climate movement.

Sergio Beltrán — better known as Yeyo — was born and raised in Mexico City and moved to Oaxaca in 1997 to support and learn from indigenous communities. Through his work he has developed a deep respect for the capacity people have to make a good life *(buen vivir)* for themselves when they are able to freely take responsibility for their own communities.

Ram Bhat is the co-founder of Maraa, an arts and media collective in India. He is currently pursuing a PhD in media and communications at the London School of Economics.

Nadine Bloch is currently Training Director for Beautiful Trouble, as well as an artist, political organizer, direct action trainer, and puppetista.

Andrew Boyd is co-founder of the Beautiful Trouble project, author of several odd books, and a long-time veteran of creative campaigns for social change. You can find him at andrewboyd.com.

Gui Bueno is a native of Brazil and completely crazy for theoretical discussions about the media, its central role in capitalism, its disadvantages and (why not?) benefits. He works for Open Knowledge Foundation Brazil where he takes care of communications (but learns much more than he communicates).

Tomaz Capobianco is an architect and researcher. While living in São Paulo, he worked with different informal communities, studying temporary autonomous zones and urban settlements such as the favela of Heliópolis.

Hope Chigudu is a Ugandan/Zimbabwean feminist activist and consultant in gender and organizational development. She is interested in coaching and supporting young leaders.

Rudo Chigudu is a Zimbabwean artist, feminist, and activist who believes in the revolutionary power of the arts for healing and fueling revolutions, and whose work in centered on the politics surrounding women's bodies. She also believes there is nothing like a dose of laughter and a pinch of madness to keep the soul alive and a revolution going.

Agness Chindimba is a feminist and a disability rights activist who is passionate about advocating for issues that affect persons with disabilities, especially women and girls because they are the most vulnerable.

Aerin Dunford is a writer, upcycling artist, process designer and facilitator, yoga instructor, and an independent process consultant using Art of Hosting and other participative approaches as a basis for her work with organizations.

Mark Engler, a writer based in Philadelphia, is an editorial board member at *Dissent,* and a contributing editor at *Yes! Magazine.* He is a co-author, with Paul Engler, of *This Is an Uprising: How Nonviolent Revolt Is Shaping the Twenty-First Century* (Nation Books).

Paul Engler is founding director of the Center for the Working Poor, based in Los Angeles, and co-founder of Momentum Training, which trains hundreds of activists each year in the principles of momentum-driven organizing. He is a co-author, with Mark Engler, of *This Is an Uprising: How Nonviolent Revolt Is Shaping the Twenty-First Century* (Nation Books).

Abraham García Gárate was a founding member of the Zapatista Caravan and a student activist in the 1990s.

Emily Hong is a feminist anthropologist, filmmaker, and co-founder of Rhiza Collective. Emily has directed several collaborative films including *Get By* (2014), *Nobel Nok Dah* (2015), and *For My Art* (2016), which have explored issues of solidarity and labor, womanhood and identity in the refugee experience, and the gendered spectatorship of performance art.

Ahmad Kassawneh is a campaign and advocacy expert, and the founder and vice secretary general of the Jordanian National Youth political party. In recent years he has managed several humanitarian and political campaigns in the Middle East and Europe, including several multi-million-dollar humanitarian fundraisers.

George Katsiaficas is a Fulbright Fellow, student of Herbert Marcuse, and long-time activist. He is the author of *The Imagination of the New Left: A Global Analysis of 1968*, and has recently published two volumes about East Asian uprisings in the 1980s and 1990s: *Asia's Unknown Uprisings* (PM Press).

Ben Leather is a campaigner on human rights and the environment at Global Witness, and also provides training for local activists on how to interact strategically with international human rights mechanisms. Follow him at @BenLeather1.

McDonald Lewanika is a social justice activist who has worked with several groups in Zimbabwe's quest for democratization. He was the founding director of the Student's Solidarity Trust, the Executive Director of the Crisis in Zimbabwe Coalition, and currently serves as the deputy chair of the Magamba Activist Network, which makes use of spoken word, stand-up comedy, and festivals as vehicles for activism.

Angeline Makore is a Zimbabwean human rights activist who is passionate about community development and defending women's and girls' rights. She is the founder of Spark READ, a youth-led initiative that seeks to address and redress challenges faced by young people in marginalized communities in Zimbabwe.

Firoze Manji is a Kenyan activist and writer, and the founder of Pambazuka News, Pambazuka Press, and Fahamu. He currently heads Pan-African Baraza, an initiative of ThoughtWorks.

Marcelo Marquesini is a socio-environmental activist and campaigner who has been operating for 20 years in the Brazilian Amazon in defense of forest conservation and indigenous and traditional communities' rights. He is also a co-founder and facilitator of Escola de Ativismo (School of Activism).

Megan Martin is a program consultant, facilitator, and community activator living and working in Latin America. As a part of the growing community of Art of Hosting facilitators and practitioners in Mexico, she has put these processes to use (along with participatory theater practices) while collaborating with NGOs, activists, businesses, governments, and civil society groups seeking stronger participation, innovation, and impact in their work.

Dave Oswald Mitchell is a writer, editor, organizer and troublemaker who divides his time between western Canada, southern Mexico, and points in-between. He serves as the Editorial Director of Beautiful Trouble.

Carolina Munis has a Bachelor's degree in International Relations and is the co-founder and a member of LGBT rights group Coletivo Transformação, which builds an autonomous, non-formal popular education experience for transgender people in São Paulo, Brazil. She is also a member of Escola de Ativismo (School of Activism).

Mahmoud Nawajaa is a Palestinian human rights activist and youth organizer. He is the General Coordinator for the Boycott, Divestment, Sanctions (BDS) National Committee, a Palestinian-led global movement.

Hellenah Okiring is a social activist, storyteller, and facilitator from Uganda who is passionate about transforming community and enabling positive change for humanity. She is the founder of the Dream Initiative for the Global Advancement of Social Arts, an organization dedicated to promoting active citizenship, leadership development, and economic justice through the use of social art and new media platforms.

Vijay Prashad is Professor of International Studies at Trinity College and Chief Editor of LeftWord Books. He is the author of eighteen books, including *The Poorer Nations: A Possible History of the Global South* (2013).

Arundhati Roy is the author of two novels, *The God of Small Things* and *The Ministry of Utmost Happiness*. Her latest works of non-fiction include *The Doctor and the Saint* and *The End of Imagination*. She lives in Delhi.

Samar Saeed is a writer based in Jordan who holds a BA from George Mason University and an MA in Near and Middle Eastern Studies with a major in Politics (Distinction) from SOAS, University of London. Her research and academic interests include the political economy of the Arab world, history, education, and culture.

Vandana Shiva is a physicist, ecofeminist, author, and activist based in Delhi.

Eric Stoner is an adjunct professor at St. Peter's College and an editor at Waging Nonviolence, a blog that covers nonviolent action around the world. His articles have appeared in *The Guardian, Mother Jones, The Nation, Sojourners, In These Times,* and the *Pittsburgh Post-Gazette,* among other publications.

Hassan Tabikh is a Lebanese writer and activist working with civil society and international NGOs in Lebanon towards achieving social justice. Hassan also campaigns for gender equality and ending violence against women.

Marcel Taminato is an anthropologist, political strategist, learning facilitator, and co-founder of Escola de Ativismo (School of Activism) in Brazil.

Nils Amar Tegmo has gone from being a graphic designer and anarcho-punk musician carrying out direct actions against Monsanto in Nepal, to a trainer of youth activists who has worked with hundreds of young people to share skills and knowledge on creative activism and strategic campaign planning. He is currently running the online learning platform and toolkit Global Change Lab.

Elspeth Tilley teaches theater and creative activism, writes (occasionally funny) plays about climate change, and lives in New Zealand.

Sophie Toupin's work explores the linkages between technology and activism. She presently works for Media@McGill, a hub for research and scholarship on media, technology, and culture at McGill University in Montreal, Quebec, Canada.

Norman Tumuhimbise is an activist and coordinator of The Jobless Brotherhood, a nonviolent Ugandan youth activist group. He is also the author of the books *Behind the Devil's Line* and *Unsowing the Mustard Seed.*

Joseph Wah (Poe Kyaw) returned to Myanmar in 2013, after working for an exiled Myanmar non-governmental organization based in Thailand, where he now works with different youth organizations and networks on a voluntary basis. He partnered with other youth in providing strategic support to student unions' protests against the National Education Law, including organizing and taking part in solidarity protests, and performing outreach and advocacy to international organizations and governments.

Søren Warburg is a dad, political organizer, strategist, facilitator, Rosa Luxemburg lover, and Operations Director of Beautiful Rising, has spent years working with social movements and activists across the globe, and holds a MA in Political Science with a focus on civil disobedience. He is currently the Strategic Advisor for ActionAid and is active with the refugee movement in Denmark and Europe.

Phil Wilmot is a consultant-trainer who has trained many communities in nonviolent action, including those trying to protect land and natural resources, end corruption, and fight unemployment.

Thinzar Shunlei Yi is a youth advocate and experienced activist, campaigner, and organizer based in Yangon, Myanmar, who initiated the first ever Myanmar Youth Forum in 2012, worked with the National Youth ASEAN Youth Forum 2014 at Yangon University, and organized the ASEAN Youth Forum 2014 at Yangon University, Myanmar. She is now working with Action Committee for Democracy Development as Advocacy Coordinator and is a coordinator at the Yangon Youth Network.

RESOURCES

ACTIVISM + ORGANIZING

Global Change Lab | *ActionAid*
globalchangelab.org
A training hub for global activists.

The Mobilisation Cookbook | *The Moblab and Greenpeace*
mobilisationlab.org/mobilisation-tools/the-mobilisation-cookbook
A guide to cooking up people-powered campaigns.

Organizing toolbox | *350.org*
trainings.350.org
Available in English, Português, Français, Deutsch.

The Barefoot Guide Connection
barefootguide.org
The Barefoot Guides compile stories, analyses, and resources from around the globe, each under a key theme.

Actipedia | *The Center for Artistic Activism and the Yes Lab*
actipedia.org
A wiki for creative activism.

Video activism resources | *Witness*
witness.org/resources
Training materials for using video to fight for human rights.
Available in five languages.

DIGITAL SECURITY

Email self-defense | *Free Software Foundation*
emailselfdefense.fsf.org
Step-by-step guide to communicating securely by email.
Available in 11 languages.

PRISM-break
prism-break.org
Directory of tools and applications for working and communicating more securely. Available in 26 languages.

Control your data: How to do it yourself
eff.org/wp/effs-top-12-ways-protect-your-online-privacy
The Me and My Shadow project helps you control your data traces, see how you're being tracked, and learn more about the data industry.

Security in a box | ***Frontline Defenders and Tactical Technology Collective***
securityinabox.org
Tools and tactics for digital security.

Surveillance self-defense | ***Electronic Frontier Foundation***
ssd.eff.org
Tips, tools, and how-tos for safer online communications. Available in 11 languages.

Holistic security | ***Tactical Tech***
holistic-security.tacticaltech.org
A strategy manual to help human rights defenders maintain their well-being in action.

MOVEMENT MEDIA

Global Voices
globalvoices.org
Citizen media stories from around the world report in 35 languages.

Open Democracy
opendemocracy.net
Independent global media platform focusing on human rights, social justice, and democracy.

Waging Nonviolence
wagingnonviolence.org
A source for original news and analysis about struggles for justice and peace around the globe.

INDEX

EDITORS:

JUMAN ABUJBARA

Lawyer and human rights defender | *Amman, Jordan*

ANDREW BOYD

Wrangler-in-Chief Emeritus of Beautiful Trouble | *New York, US*

DAVE OSWALD MITCHELL

Editorial Director of Beautiful Trouble | *Regina, Canada*

MARCEL TAMINATO

Co-founder of the Escola de Ativismo | *São Paulo, Brazil*

PROJECT COORDINATOR:

SØREN WARBURG

ActionAid | *Copenhagen*

EDITORIAL DIRECTOR:

DAVE MITCHELL

Beautiful Trouble | *Saskatchewan*

COPY EDITOR:

MARA RANVILLE

Beautiful Trouble | *New York*

TRANSLATION TEAM:

ZULAIKHA ABURISHA | Arabic language editor | *Amman*

ANDREA BELLARUTI | Spanish language editor | *Oaxaca*

MOHAMED ABDEL-HAMID | Arabic translator | *Halifax*

FAREED EL SHANTORY | Arabic translator | *Cairo*

CAMILA MENA | Spanish translator | *Santiago*

MARÍA JULIANA ZAPATA | Spanish translator | *Bogotá*

CAROLINA MUNIS | Portuguese editor | *São Paulo*

TRAINING DIRECTOR:

NADINE BLOCH | Beautiful Trouble | *Washington, D.C.*

JAM SESSION FACILITATION:

RAE ABILEAH, JUMAN ABUJBARA, SERGIO BELTRÁN, NADINE BLOCH, THEIS DENKER, NISREEN HAJ AHMAD, DAVE MITCHELL, GRACE RUVIMBO CHIRENJE, FRANCIS RWODZI, MEGAN MARTIN, MARCEL TAMINATO, SOREN WARBURG, PHIL WILMOT, SUZAN WILMOT, THINZAR SHUNLEI YI

ART DIRECTION AND BOOK DESIGN:

CRISTIAN FLEMING | Creative Director of Beautiful Trouble and Principal at The Public Society | *New York*

DIANA HAJ AHMAD | Art Direction | The Public Society | *New York*

JOSIAH WERNING | Book Design | The Public Society | *New York*

TECH TEAM:

ADRIAN CARPENTER | Master Coder | *Oakland*

PHILLIP SMITH | CTO of Beautiful Trouble | *Vancouver*

ADVISORY NETWORK

Our Advisory Network gathers together people with a variety of skill sets and working contexts to act as a hub of expertise to inform project decisions.

NISREEN HAJ AHMAD

Co-founder of AHEL & Mujtama3i and board member of Leading Change Network | *Amman*

KATHARINE AINGER

Co-editor of *We Are Everywhere: The Irresistible Rise of Global Anti-Capitalism* and former co-editor of New Internationalist | *Barcelona*

TOM ALLEN

Ocean Lovers Project Lead for Greenpeace and digital expert with an in-depth knowledge of the third sector | *Sydney*

KARA ANDRADE

Journalist, entrepreneur, multimedia producer, and PhD student at the School of Communication at American University | *Washington, D.C.*

JUDITH DEMBETEMBE CHIYANGWA

Director and co-founder of The Girls Legacy | *Harare*

LAURA WALKER MCDONALD

Chief Executive Officer for Social Impact Lab (creators of FrontlineSMS, award-winning open-source software used in over 135 countries) | *Washington, D.C.*

AURELIA MOSER

Developer and code-cartographer at Ushahidi and Internews-Kenya | *Nairobi and New York*

GABI SOBLIYE

Programme Coordinator for Tactical Technology Collective | *Berlin*

PHIL WILMOT

Board member at Solidarity Uganda | *Kampala*

SUZAN ABONG WILMOT

Team of Directors for Solidarity Uganda | *Kampala*

THINZAR SHUNLEI YI

Coordinator of Burma's National Youth Congress and the Yangon Youth Network, Advocacy Coordinator for Action Committee for Democracy Development | *Yangon*